D1534951

THE OUTSIDE CHANCE
of Maximilian Glick

A Novel by Morley Torgov

LESTER
&ORPEN
DENNYS
PUBLISHERS

Also by Morley Torgov
A Good Place to Come From
The Abramsky Variations

Acknowledgements
Once again to Beverley Slopen and Helen Mathé; also to Janet Hamilton Engel and the Ontario Arts Council.

Canadian Cataloguing in Publication Data

Torgov, Morley, 1928-
    The outside chance of Maximilian Glick

ISBN 0-919630-29-4

I. Title.

PS8589.073097   C813'.54   C82-094529-3
PR9199.3.T67097

Design by Green Graphics
Production by Paula Chabanais Productions
Typesetting by Compeer Typographic Services Limited

Printed and bound in Canada by
The Hunter Rose Company for
Lester & Orpen Dennys Ltd.
78 Sullivan Street
Toronto, Ontario
M5T 1C1

To Anna Pearl, Sarah Jane and Alexander

Part One

1

As a rule, June evenings in Steelton, though softened here and there with the promise of summer, retained just enough sharpness to remind one that in this stony section of the north, winter camped no farther away than the dark lines of firs that encircled the small city. Elsewhere, in temperate places, spring had bravely proclaimed its arrival weeks earlier. But here it was still obliged to keep its voice to a whisper, for winter — whose truces were never reliable — might awaken at any moment, as if summoned by some ungodly bugle, and march yet again on the town, paying little or no heed to timeliness and tradition.

The evenings, like the mornings, began and ended in questions. Should one venture out for a stroll? Try out a new casting rod on the banks of the St. Anne River? Paint the backyard fence? Or was it wiser just to stay put behind the evening paper, avoiding all confrontations with nature? Even the bibulous drifters, greedily inhaling the beery perfume that wafted from the entranceways of the taverns, couldn't make up their minds whether to panhandle indoors or out. Either way was a gamble.

In a time of extreme indecision, one family in Steelton had its evening's work clearly cut out. The family of Maximilian Glick — his parents Henry and Sarah, and grandparents Augustus and Bryna Glick — were locked in debate over the boy's future profession, a subject of contention since the days of his first halting steps, charged now with a sense of urgency because he would soon become three and time was flying!

Henry Glick, extolling his son's prowess with knife and fork, insisted that the boy was a born surgeon. "You can see it in his hands," he said.

Grandfather Glick, acknowledging the boy's dexterity, argued nevertheless that "Maximilian Glick" would look far better on the door of a large law firm, preferably at the head of the list. "Maybe," said the boy's grandfather, his old eyes watery, "I will live long enough, God willing, to refer to my grandson as Judge Glick."

To the boy's mother, Maximilian possessed all the qualities of a scientist — alertness, inquisitiveness, a gift for numbers. In her son she saw nothing less than another Einstein, one who would fulfill her dream of altering certain natural laws hitherto considered unalterable: the tendency of cigarette smoke to rise, dust to settle, down-filled chesterfields to acquire unsightly rump-marks, neighborhood dogs always to convene on her front lawn when there were at least ten others handy.

"You're all crazy!" said Bryna Glick. "For all we know, Maximilian may choose to hole up in some cave and write books." The others dismissed the idea as preposterous. "Is that the best you can come up with?" old Augustus scoffed. "A man needs a *real* profession. *Books* he can always write in his spare time."

"I just want my grandchild to grow up like any normal child," said Bryna Glick, refusing to back down. "The poor boy hasn't even finished making his quota of mudpies yet!"

Once again Bryna Glick, erect, white-haired, peppery despite her years and delicate physique, was playing the role of her grandson's champion. Not that the boy was ever abused. On the contrary, there existed an ongoing family contest — she herself was a regular participant — to determine who could do more for Maximilian, who could give more, amuse more, protect more, love more. In such an overpowering atmosphere, at least one benefactor had to break ranks occasionally to speak for the beneficiary; *some*one had to reduce to reasonable proportions everyone's vast expectations of him.

This was a role to which Bryna Glick had appointed herself even before Maximilian was born, one for which she felt especially equipped. She too had once been an only child, eagerly awaited, late in coming. From experience she understood how parental love, too long in ferment, could transform the gentlest shelter into a maximum security lockup, one no child could hope to escape. Bryna had kept her premonitions strictly to herself all during Sarah's pregnancy. Anyway, who wanted to listen?

Her husband, Augustus, would say — misunderstanding his wife: "Trouble with you is, you don't understand how much this baby is wanted."

Bryna would retaliate by suggesting her husband go soak his head. "Of course I understand," she would counter. "*Everyone in Steelton understands!*"

The fact was, everyone — well, almost everyone — *did* understand.

Henry and Sarah Glick had been married just over ten years, and though by no means old — they were barely middle-aged, in fact, when their one and only child was born — they had begun to think that it was not in their stars to make a child. In small cities like Steelton, where the Glick family lived and prospered, any couple that fails to produce at least one heir in ten years of marriage becomes a popular subject of speculation. Some friends and acquaintances had guessed that the trouble with Henry and Sarah was that, though bright, when it came to having a baby they simply didn't know how. Others said they knew how but not when. Still others gossiped that they knew when but not why. And Morris Moskover, known as the Local Sage because he could take any fact, add water, and come up with an instant opinion, said the trouble with Henry and Sarah Glick was that they knew how, when, and why . . . but not where!

Perhaps the Local Sage was right, for soon after their first visit to Europe (which included five nights in Paris) Henry and Sarah received the happy news: some months later, and several weeks overdue, their son was born. "The ten most-wanted fugitives in the land *together* aren't wanted half as much as this baby!" proclaimed Morris Moskover. This too was accurate, proving once again that being a sage has nothing to do with brains.

The air Maximilian Glick breathed was saturated with love, like the air of a forest in spring, of a seaside in summer. The child was loved from the moment his first cries bounced off the white tile walls of the operating room at Steelton General and into the ears of his unbelieving mother; loved by his father, his grandparents, their friends, by relatives who, living hundreds of miles away, sent telegrams of congratulation. Even the Roman Catholic nursing sisters, blinding white in their habits, hovered over his bassinette like overgrown doves, cooing adjectives of praise, as if he were the infant Moses neatly packaged in the bullrushes.

On the eighth day of his life, the boy underwent circumcision, the ritual prescribed for Jewish male infants; then he was named in keeping with ancient custom, receiving his Hebrew name first, followed by his "English" name, after which he let out a wail that pierced Steelton General from one end to the other, and could be heard clear out to the parking lot.

To the boy's grandfather, the child's outcry was a sign that the decline and fall of the West was complete. "There's no excuse for this kind of thing in the twentieth century," he muttered, shaking his head worriedly. Augustus Glick was referring to the practice of performing circumcisions without anaesthetic.

But to Bryna Glick, it was the *name* so ceremoniously bestowed on her grandson that was inexcusable in the twentieth century. "Wouldn't *you* kick up a fuss," she protested to Augustus, "if you were facing a lifetime of being called Maximilian? With a name like that, a boy begins life as an adult, full of problems."

Days before, when the question of the name arose, Bryna

had registered her disapproval. "It sounds more like something you'd stick on a battleship ... just before it sinks!"

"I'll thank you to remember," said her husband, "that Maximilian was one of the great kings of Bavaria." The old man drew himself up like a soldier. "My great-grandfather served with distinction in his Department of Household Supply!"

"You mean he carried sacks of coal into the palace basement, don't you?" said his wife.

Undaunted by the truth, old Augustus Glick went on: "My grandfather and father, rest in peace, bore the name Maximilian with pride."

Bryna Glick had heard this story many times, and at this point in her life was thoroughly unimpressed. "Caesar was one of Rome's greatest emperors," she retorted, "but the only thing named after him these days is a salad!"

Bryna Glick knew that people didn't want to pick their way through ten letters and four syllables just to get to a person's surname. Before the boy can walk, she told herself, he'll be called Maxie, and before he's learned to count to a hundred the world will be calling him Max. No matter what, it was no name to hang on a youngster in this day and age.

Grandmother Glick was thinking mostly of her husband's late Uncle Max from Chicago. Uncle Max was short, and his bald head — too large for his body — looked as if it had been dropped into place by a not-too-gentle Providence; the man had no neck, at least none that was visible, and his fat face surrounded a cigar day and night. Uncle Max spent most of his life as a traveling salesman. Whenever he arrived in town, he and the clothes on his back, the neckties in his sample cases — even the sample cases! — reeked of stale cigar smoke. After his departure, any hotel room Uncle Max occupied had to be sealed off like an isolation ward. When he laughed, which was often because he was fond of repeating off-color stories picked up on the road, his cigar never left the center of his face. No, Max was definitely the wrong name for a little boy.

But uncles and the twentieth century aside, Henry Glick, with Sarah at his side nodding approval, settled the argument. "I'll bet there isn't another person with a name even *close* to it within a thousand miles of Steelton." Henry brought his fist down like a gavel. "If it's a boy . . . it's Maximilian." Eyeing his mother, he added: "Case closed!"

It was the first in a long succession of causes Bryna pleaded — and lost — over the next few years. Because the youngster wasn't always capable of articulating what was on his mind, his grandmother jumped at every opportunity to present his case — or the case she imagined he was trying to make in a household where, it seemed, everything said or done was governed by some form of regulation.

There were, of course, all sorts of edicts concerning tooth-brushing, foot-wiping, television viewing, nose-blowing. Then decrees of a higher order: yesterday's newspaper was never thrown out until Sarah's crossword was completed and Henry had read the stock market page. (One did not interrupt during these rituals.) Lights were generally turned off in one room before they were turned on in another. Bicycles were never ridden on Tuesdays and Fridays until the garbage had been put out for collection. Toilets were called washrooms; supper was called dinner, especially when company was present. Those who wasted not in this world, wanted not. Stitches in time saved nine, except in the Glick household where they were expected to save at least ten.

At the same time, Maximilian's defaults and delinquencies necessarily increased until they lay on his slim shoulders like the national debt. And always, it was Bryna Glick standing up for his rights, attacking, arguing, supplicating, often losing her temper, usually losing her case.

One day, just before Maximilian's eighth birthday, Bryna Glick at last came in from the cold.

Unlike her husband, who was born into a sober, nose-to-the-grindstone family of Viennese merchants, Bryna had come from a modest but cheerful home in Odessa, a city in Russia where it seemed every second person was an artist or musician. Her mother had taught piano, her father was a violinist in an orchestra. Their apartment, small and crammed with furniture and books, constantly teemed with people tuning instruments, arguing heatedly about the correct way to play some musical phrase or other, humming melodic passages and tapping out rhythms with a fury, as musicians do when they're sure they're right and everybody else is wrong.

And it was because of this background that Bryna declared one day: "Maxie will be eight before we know it. It's high time the boy took music lessons."

For one brief incredible moment unanimity reigned in the Glick family (excluding Maximilian who was off somewhere on his bike at the time).

But then, the question: What instrument should he learn to play?

"Piano," said Henry, "that's the ideal instrument for a surgeon. Nothing keeps the fingers in shape like a piano. I'm sure we can find a good upright somewhere in town. After he graduates medical school I'll buy him a proper grand."

"A man ought to play a *wind* instrument," said Augustus Glick. "When I was a boy, one of the finest trombonists in Austria was a judge, of all people ... Judge Wilhelm von Finkenstein. Superb musician. Very conceited judge. Whenever he took time off from court to practise, everyone within hearing said, 'There goes von Finkenstein blowing his own horn again.' There's something about wind instruments; they seem to go hand in hand with the legal profession. If I had my way, I'd start Maxie on a trumpet."

"Anyone can bang on a keyboard or blow through a tube," Sarah now said, "but to draw music from a string takes more than manual dexterity or a good set of lungs; you need a precise mind, the mind of a scientist." Still convinced her son was another Einstein, she thought he should begin lessons on the violin.

"What about letting Maxie choose for himself?" Bryna said.

"With all due respect, Mother —" (Sarah Glick always

addressed the older woman in this manner during war games; it was her spear.) "With all due respect, what if he chooses the kazoo?"

"Sarah dear — " ("Sarah dear" was Bryna Glick's spear, tipped in a not-too-mild solution of acid.) "Sarah dear, don't be such a snob."

Within the week the issue was resolved. Into Henry Glick's furniture store shambled the notorious ne'er-do-well, Doc Ingoldsby, said to be older than Steelton itself. Called "Doc" because he boasted an honorary degree in geology (which nobody had ever laid eyes on), Ingoldsby inhabited an unworked farm a few miles from town where he spent his days sitting on his front porch corroding like an old battery. Back in the Thirties his mining company had made and lost a fortune. Little by little ever since, Doc Ingoldsby had been forced to sell off his personal possessions to sustain himself and a procession of wives who paraded in and out of his bed and his heart, leaving him virtually bankrupt. The Glicks had become steady customers, sometimes out of pure compassion, occasionally because some item — an antique desk, a rare vase — truly appealed to them or might be resold at a profit.

Doffing a greasy derby hat, setting down his walking stick, Doc Ingoldsby smiled slyly. "Henry Glick," he called out, rubbing his hands together, "this is your lucky day. Ever heard of a Bechstein?"

"A Bechstein? No. What is it, something you drink out of?"

Ingoldsby's body shook like a condemned building, and a rasping noise emanated from somewhere inside his throat. He was laughing. "Good God, man," he cried, "you've never heard of a Bechstein?"

"Never."

Ingoldsby pointed to the telephone behind Henry. "Get on that contraption, young fella, and call your dear mother. I betcha all the fish in the St. Anne River *she* knows what I'm talkin' about."

The old man easily won his bet. "Of course I know," said

Bryna. "Bechsteins were made in Germany years and years ago. Maybe they're still making them, for all I know. Some of the finest pianos in the world. Why do you ask?"

"I'll tell you later. I haven't time now," said Henry.

On the following day — Max's eighth birthday — a van pulled into the driveway of the Glick residence and two men with arms like wrestlers' inched a giant old upright piano out of the back of the truck, up the front steps of the house, and into a corner of the livingroom that had been cleared to receive it.

Scarcely had the brawny pair set the instrument in place when Bryna Glick was seated at the keyboard playing a simple C-major scale, first with one hand, then with both, laughing with all the delight of a young girl in that human beehive in long-ago Odessa. And Maximilian's mother, polish and soft cloth in hand, was already removing tarnish from the brass candlesticks that protruded from the carved cornerposts.

Soon Maximilian's father and grandfather showed up and all four were crowded around the Bechstein, running their fingertips over its richly grained mahogany, pounding out ambitious but clumsy chords and arpeggios on the slightly yellowed ivory keys, and congratulating themselves and each other for having the foresight, the luck, the wisdom — the plain horse-sense — to acquire the instrument.

At which point Maximilian Glick returned home from school.

"Surprise ... surprise!"

"Happy birthday!"

He looked at four beaming, loving faces; then his eyes fell on the object behind.

And Maximilian Glick, just into his ninth year of life, wanting in his young heart nothing more than a model Boeing 747 — the one with battery-powered wing lights flashing on and off, and engines whining as if ready for take-off — Maximilian Glick found himself led to a monstrous piano, a dark spooky form that reminded him of the sacrificial altar he'd seen recently in a horror movie.

"Happy birthday, Maximilian," said his father.

Old Augustus Glick wiped a tear from the corner of his eye. "Many happy returns, Maximilian."

Max's mother kissed him first where the dark wavy hair on his head was parted, then again on the bridge of his neatly shaped nose, which made him squint. "It's not a violin," she said, "but at least it's got strings, Maxie."

And Bryna Glick, swollen with happiness because to her a house without music was a body without blood, bent down and kissed him on the cheek. "Max," she glowed, "it was my idea. Someday, when you're a fine musician like your great-grandfather and great-grandmother in Russia, you'll thank me for this."

On the birthday cake, carried proudly into the diningroom by Max's mother, it seemed to the boy that there were not eight but *eighty* candles all burning brightly. For suddenly Maximilian Glick felt old, much older than his years.

Henry Glick had opened a bottle of wine for this festive occasion, and for the first time Max was permitted a small glass all to himself.

"A toast," said the boy's father. The adults at the table raised their glasses. "To Maximilian!"

"To Maximilian!" said his grandfather.

"To Maxie!" said his mother.

There was a pause. At last Grandmother Glick, still aglow, raised her glass a bit higher than the others. "To Max!" she said.

The boy managed a smile. With his elders gazing down on him, he brought his wine glass to his lips and took a sip, all the while keeping his eyes on the one person in the circle responsible for this betrayal. How could you do this to me? he asked silently. How *could* you?

Maximilian Glick was looking directly at his grandmother, at Bryna Glick.

While the others lingered over the dinnertable, arguing as usual about what their son and grandson ought to be when he grew up, Max, having excused himself, went out onto the front porch and sat on a step. With his back against a thick wooden spindle that supported the handrail, he surveyed the world around him.

The Glick house was situated on the crown of Pine Hill, the highest section of Steelton, a city in northern Ontario of fifty thousand or so inhabitants. It was an old red brick house, built some fifty years earlier by Augustus Glick, not long after he and Bryna had settled in what was then a town of a few thousand. Max's father was born in that house. Eventually Augustus retired from the furniture business he had founded, leaving it in Henry's capable hands. The elder Glicks moved into an apartment downtown, not large but modern and comfortable, with a balcony that overlooked the St. Anne, and Max's parents took over the old house in time for the arrival of their infant son.

A wide porch, painted white with gunmetal trim, ran the length of the house. From that vantage point one could take in the city below.

The west end of town was dominated by the steel plant. By day the plant sprawled like a gathering of dragons, belching smoke and fire. At night the dragons breathed flames into the velvety sky, turning it red. In the clear still air of this night, the smoke from the plant rose straight up until it seemed to Max that soot would soon cover the moon.

To the east there was the harbor, bustling with lake freighters. At this hour their shapes were indistinguishable, appearing to Max as long strings of lights, some heading upriver in the direction of Duluth or Thunder Bay, others downbound for Detroit and Cleveland, places Max had heard about, places he yearned to see. Occasionally the ships would signal to each other with short sharp blasts of their horns; otherwise they moved in total silence.

At the center of the panorama stood downtown Steelton, block after block of buildings of questionable architectural parentage arranged around the junction of King Street and Queen Street. In their prime, King and Queen were hot-blooded rivals for the town's commerce. Recently, however, the pulse had begun to weaken in these avenues as first one, then another, shopping center opened on the outskirts of town. With the exception of the odd hardy entrepreneur — like Max's father — most of the downtown merchants had gone to asphalt pastures in the suburbs, leaving King and Queen to the city's institutions.

The most noble of these were the banks, small-scale replicas of Greek temples, erected in an earlier time when depositors equated security and integrity with fluted pillars. There were insurance and financial and real estate offices with plain no-nonsense façades that could have been designed only by a committee of carpenters. The two local movie houses, battered victims of television and suburban living, huddled for comfort beside each other on King Street, their once-proud marquees shorn because of a municipal ordinance against overhangs. By contrast, the Y.M.C.A. and the Memorial Arena stood their ground directly across the street, as if to demonstrate that there were still muscle and energy left in the old ward. Thanks to the presence of Steelton General Hospital and a row of doctors' offices and pharmacies, several blocks of Queen were as antiseptic as any public thoroughfare could be. But next door to Healing dwelt Justice, a germ-laden courthouse built in the latter days of Queen Victoria, which sat on its treeless lot looking very much like the old lady herself — stolid, crusty, and humorless.

At least once a year — usually around New Year's Eve — in one or another of the town's bars, chairs would still fly and glassware scatter like shrapnel over nothing more important than which street — King or Queen — was the main one. But one fact about their intersection was undisputed: it was clearly the most chaotic in all of Steelton. Traffic jams, non-existent anywhere else in town, occurred with regularity at King and Queen every weekday at five, as millworkers streaming east along King locked car horns with downtown officeworkers streaming west, all of them intending to proceed north on Queen to suburban homes in the hill sections. As one depended upon the law of gravity, one could rely on the traffic lights at that intersection to be out of order in

winter (usually the result of iced-up powerlines or a delin-
quent snowball aimed expertly at a red light). In summer the
pavement would be torn up; Steelton's City Council was forever opening, closing, and reopening gaping craters in that
portion of the roadway as part of some grand vision of sewage disposal to which the mayor and his aldermen had, like
crusaders, dedicated themselves.

One of the last retailers on King Street, not far from its
intersection with Queen, was A. Glick & Son. The largest furniture store in these parts, A. Glick & Son ("Est. 1924") catered
to every taste. Among its patrons were elderly couples who
decorated their modest bungalows with too many doilies,
china cats, and velvet cushions bearing scenes of palm trees
and full moons set against black skies. Young couples too
could find what they wanted at Glick's — the up-to-the-
minute furnishings which, like their fantasies, were "in" one
day and "out" the next. Some Saturdays, if there was nothing
better to do, Maximilian would roam among the rows of chesterfields and rocking chairs and end-tables pretending that
they were planes lined up in a hangar, and that he could
choose any one and be off into the skies in minutes. Secretly
he wished Henry Glick were the captain of a jetliner, and he
its co-pilot.

Except for the distant toot now and then from the steel
plant, or the sound of freight cars being shunted to and fro in
the railyards running parallel to the river, all of Steelton lay
silent now. From inside the house came murmurs that told
Maximilian his future was probably still being debated over
the dinnertable, as if nothing else in Steelton, or all the world,
mattered. And glancing over his shoulder, he could see through
the livingroom window the upper structure of the old Bechstein,
a dark cloud over the horizon.

And for the first time the thought occurred to Maximilian:
one could be surrounded by love, security, comfort — but
still feel lonely. What was more, the boy couldn't recall a
time when he'd felt more like a Maximilian, burdened with
becoming an adult before his time.

On the following day, at the start of Maximilian's Hebrew lesson, Rabbi Kaminsky, his teacher — who'd been spiritual leader of Steelton's Jewish community for over twenty years and knew everything that went on in the lives of its people — extended his hand and smiled. "Well, Maxileh, let me shake the hand of the next Horowitz."

"Who's Horowitz?"

"What, you've never heard of Horowitz ... probably the greatest pianist that ever lived? There are many outstanding piano players in this world, Maxileh, but there's only one Horowitz!"

The boy took Rabbi Kaminsky's hand with no show of enthusiasm. As far as Maximilian Glick was concerned, unless this Horowitz had piloted an X-15 to Mars and back without stopping for lunch, the name was of very little interest.

Rabbi Kaminsky, a perceptive man, nodded his head. "Don't despair, Maximilian," he said. "Sometimes God has a habit of dropping pianos on us. But other times ... other times He parts the waters of the Red Sea!"

All the way home from that Hebrew lesson, Maximilian thought about the parting of the Red Sea, and that evening he once again sat alone on the front porch, his back pressed against the handrail spindles, looking up at the sky. A minute or two earlier the sun had disappeared, as if sucked down the enormous smokestacks of the steel plant, but there were just enough rays left to paint the trail of a jetliner passing high overhead, turning it to bright silver against the darkening blue. Max imagined for a moment that the sky was a sea and that the airliner — almost invisible now — was parting it, permitting the passengers within to pass to some promised land: a place where, in the shadows of tall skyscrapers, in the tide of human beings that swept along the sidewalks of a metropolis, a boy like him could do what a boy wanted most to — make his own choices.

"Someday ... someday ..." Maximilian Glick, his eyes on the vanishing remnant of jet trail, whispered to himself. "I must get out. I must get out. I *will* get out!"

2

It fell to Bryna Glick as the family's senior advisor on cultural matters to recommend a piano teacher for Maximilian. But the moment she announced her choice, the family's junior advisor on such matters, her daughter-in-law, objected vehemently.

"What!" said Sarah Glick. "Deliver an innocent eight-year-old into the hands of that ... that disgusting man! Everyone in town knows Derek Blackthorn is never more than six inches from a bottle of gin ... even in his sleep!"

"What goes through the man's kidneys is of no importance to me, Sarah dear."

"With all due respect, Mother, you must be blind to the man's personal life. Totally blind."

"Really, Sarah dear? What else have I overlooked?"

"I've never seen him without a cigarette dangling out of a corner of his mouth. And God only knows what else he smokes in that house of his."

"I'm not interested in his lungs either, Sarah dear."

"I doubt if he's taken a bath since the day he landed in Steelton."

"He takes long walks in the rain instead," said Bryna Glick. "That's good enough for me."

Controversies of this sort were not unusual between Bryna and Sarah Glick. Whenever one chose to be prosecutor, the other automatically elected to act as defense counsel. According to their husbands, who found themselves regularly pressed into jury duty, the two women actually thrived on this adversary system; it was their continuing source of energy, their own peculiar fountain of youth.

"With all due respect, Mother," Sarah Glick went on, refusing to retreat, "there are at least a half-dozen better piano teachers in Steelton."

"Tidier, Sarah dear ... not better."

"Tidiness and talent go hand in hand — "

"Maybe when it comes to interior decorators — "

"Pablo Picasso was no interior decorator, and his studio was absolutely spotless."

"That was only when he was old," said Bryna, "and turning out doodles nobody could understand."

"Doodles! Why, Pablo Picasso died a multi-millionaire!"

"Maybe so, Sarah dear, but he never got a cent of *my* money."

Sarah Glick covered her eyes with her hands. "My God," was all she could manage, in a small voice.

"Now listen, Sarah," Bryna Glick closed in. "Like it or not, Derek Blackthorn happens to be the best piano teacher in northern Ontario. One of his pupils won a scholarship last year to the Toronto Conservatory, Amy Czerczewski — her father's a steelworker at the plant — and the talk is that the girl's on her way to the top ... New York! It's a fact too that Derek Blackthorn's uncle was Sir Basil Blackthorn, the man who conducted the Philharmonic in London, England, back in the Forties."

"I don't care if his uncle was Ludwig van Beethoven," said Maximilian's mother, "he's not a fit person to have around a young impressionable boy like Maxie."

It was common knowledge in Steelton (where very little was ever secret from anybody) that Derek Blackthorn's house down by the St. Anne River, near the harbor, was one house that would never be featured in *Better Homes and Gardens*. For one thing, Blackthorn and his wife, in addition to being prodigious smokers and drinkers, were as uninterested in good housekeeping as one could be without having one's dwelling condemned by civic officials. And then, neither of them really cared what people thought. Visitors to their house reported that it was a two-storey ashtray. Like the late Uncle Max from Chicago, the Blackthorns reeked of tobacco smoke and their fingers were stained yellow from years of accumulating nicotine.

Shizuko Blackthorn (often called "Madam Butterfly" behind her back by some of the more cultured locals) was from somewhere in the Orient — most people thought the Philippines or Japan, though she preferred to say San Francisco because apparently there was some question about whether or not she had entered Canada legally. She was a potter; she turned out bowls and vases of all sizes and shapes, and tea kettles with wicker handles, which she sold through a local craft shop. Marveling at the delicate beauty of her work, people wondered at the Blackthorn residence, which looked as though a tornado had struck the place once a day, every day, since the day ten years ago when the tall angular Englishman and his short wiry wife had moved in.

Questions were raised in well-kept livingrooms from one end of town to the other as to whether or not the strange pair was really married. (Max, who heard the questions, never got to hear the answers; every time the topic came up in his presence, his parents and their friends suddenly began to converse in the eternal language of secrecy — Yiddish — a language young Max had not yet learned to speak or understand.)

For all these reasons, Sarah Glick once again said flatly that she didn't want any son of hers exposed to the likes of Derek Blackthorn, good teacher or not. But Bryna Glick stood firm. "We are hiring Mr. Blackthorn to be Max's piano teacher, not his spiritual guide," she said.

Maximilian — a third member of the all-male jury (but without voting rights) — heard this last statement with some relief, for in Rabbi Kaminsky the boy had a friend, a man he considered his soulmate.

With fewer than twenty-five Jewish families in Steelton,

there was only a handful of Jewish children who required instruction in the Hebrew faith and language. This they received every afternoon at cheder, a special class held after regular school hours in the tiny brick-and-stucco synagogue in the old section of Steelton near the City Hall. One would think that the children, having put behind them a normal day of schooling, would resent an hour of cheder before they went home to their suppers. But not so. Rabbi Kaminsky was a good-natured man, about the same age as Augustus Glick, outwardly a bit formal but with a soul as warm as a bowl of porridge. When he told stories from the Old Testament, it was as if he'd been alive in biblical times and had personally witnessed all the miracles and catastrophes of Jewish history, so passionate and colorful was his delivery. He was clean-shaven except for a neat mustache that peeked out from under his nose. His suits were always pressed and spotless, his dark gray homburg (which he wore at all times except, presumably, to bed) always well-brushed. Everything about him — his measured walk, the way he sat (making certain to flick the knees of his trousers to preserve the crease and prevent bagging), the way he brought a teacup to his lips — was dignified, in the manner of an ambassador at court. He had a powerful baritone voice. "When *he* chants, God listens!" his congregants said.

To Maximilian Glick, it sounded as though Derek Blackthorn and Rabbi Kaminsky were born and raised on different planets. From what he'd heard thus far in the debate between his mother and grandmother, he was prepared to dislike this fellow Blackthorn immediately, even though he'd never laid eyes on the man. Anyway, thought Max, who would want to trust his grandmother's judgment? Was she not the one who'd gotten him into all this? Life *could* have been so simple. A model Boeing 747 — that's all the boy had really wanted. Was that too much to ask of four adults, one of whom — his father — ran the largest furniture store in the whole of northern Ontario?

In the end, Bryna Glick won out. Perhaps it was the good

fortune of the Czerczewski girl that decided it, but more likely it was that Max's mother Sarah liked two things in her house — peace and order.

Order she achieved by seeing to it that every corner of the fine old house shone. Henry Glick liked to say that the reason he fell in love with Sarah Nashman at college was that she was the only girl he'd met who looked forward to doing floors and windows. There wasn't a wax, a polish, a compound, or a soap with which even the young Sarah hadn't been on intimate terms.

Peace she achieved by giving in whenever an issue threatened a serious rip in the family fabric. Argue she would, and hotly too, when she thought she was right, and even when she suspected she might be wrong. But if the contest came to a stalemate, Sarah Glick's white flag went up slowly over her trench. Anyway, she told herself, a good soldier knew that the real objective of the day was to survive until tomorrow. The trick was to repair the face of defeat with the cosmetics of honorable withdrawal. Besides, there would be other sunrises over other battlefields; she knew that too.

So that is what Sarah Glick finally did. "All right Mother, I give up. You win," she said to Bryna Glick, throwing up her hands in a gesture of surrender.

Bryna and Sarah bestowed gracious smiles on each other. And two of the jurors grinned with satisfaction. Only the third — the one without a vote — remained sober, sober as the face of Judge Wilhelm von Finkenstein.

3

It was true, all true, Maximilian Glick told himself as he took
in the Blackthorn household that first Saturday morning; the
place *was* a two-storey ashtray. Unlike his own house, this
and its grab-bag contents offered evidence of neglect no matter where one's eyes fell — not ordinary neglect but a condition of carelessness achieved only through diligent effort.
Nothing seemed to be in place, or to match anything. The
pictures on the walls weren't level with the floors, which
weren't level with the ceilings. Two cats roamed freely over
furniture, books, dishes, so freely one would have thought
they held the mortgage on the premises. (One, a pitch-black
cat, was called "Spot"; the other, a wary female that never
ventured outdoors, was "Rover.") It was as if the Blackthorns
had hired a staff to come in regularly and *un*clean the house.

Two things in the Blackthorn livingroom did seem to have
escaped ramshackledom: a grand piano in the bay window
and a framed photograph of Derek Blackthorn perched atop
a tall narrow bookcase where Spot and Rover couldn't possibly
knock it over. The piano was old; Maximilian reckoned it was
at least as old as his Bechstein at home. But its mahogany
surface shone like a mirror and the ivory of its keys was
creamy to the eye, and even creamier to the touch.

The photograph of Blackthorn, set in a handsome tooled-
leather frame, showed him wearing the uniform of a pilot,
posing at the nose of an aircraft (which greatly surprised the
boy). "Yes, Maximilian, that *is* me, believe it or not," said

Blackthorn matter-of factly, sensing his new pupil's astonishment.

"*You* were in the air force?"

"Yes, the Royal Air Force. World War Two."

"What kind of plane is that?"

"Spitfire. Best fighter ever built. None better. Germans wished they'd had 'em."

"Did you shoot down any enemy planes?"

"Well, let's just say I got to fire a few rounds of ammunition now and then. Until July 23, 1944. That was the day *I* got shot down. Over Malta. Landed in the Mediterranean. Spent a few hours in the sea, thrashing about and making a complete fool of myself. Got awfully waterlogged. Thought I was finished."

"And then you were rescued?"

"Yes, by an American destroyer. Pure unadulterated luck. Made up my mind after that experience to avoid two things in life: war and water." Seating himself at the piano, Blackthorn plunged his fingers into the keyboard, producing an ear-splitting G-major chord, as if punctuating his war record once and for all. "And now, enough about my glorious past. Let's get down to your questionable future, Mr. Glick."

He motioned the boy to be seated beside him at the grand piano. "Do you know how to find middle C, Maximilian?"

"Yes." The boy pointed instantly to the key.

Blackthorn looked displeased. "How about G-sharp?"

"Haven't a clue," Maximilian confessed.

"Splendid Max, splendid." His face brightened immediately. "Then I *am* superior to you, after all. For a moment I was afraid I had another precocious young snot on my hands."

Blackthorn placed a hand on Maximilian's shoulder. "Mr. Glick, you and I are going to make music together. No doubt about it. Can you keep a secret from your chums?"

"Yes — "

"Good." Blackthorn laid an index finger — a long bony index finger with a distinct yellowish tinge along its length — on one of the keys. "*That* . . . is G-sharp. Now you play the note."

Oh well, Maximilian told himself, if one had to take piano lessons, it was far better to take them from a man who was once shot down over the Mediterranean.

Maximilian Glick set his own index finger, so short, so pale, so innocent-looking by comparison, upon the same key and pressed down.

The first note. Of the first lesson.

By the time Maximilian Glick was eleven it was clear he had the makings of a real musician. His fingers found their way up and down the Bechstein's keyboard with remarkable confidence and accuracy. He could sight-read a new piece of music almost as quickly as he could the headlines in the *Steelton Daily Star.* Because of the boy's mathematical bent, Derek Blackthorn started him on harmony, theory, and counterpoint sooner than most, and promised Grandmother Glick that before long her grandson would be ready for an elementary course in composition.

It was just as well that young Maximilian Glick had the makings of a real musician, because there was one thing he did *not* have — the makings of a real athlete.

In the school gymnasium, all of the dexterity, the quickness, the concentration he displayed at the piano, or over a problem in arithmetic or science, abandoned him, as if an electric current had been switched off. Nobody was quite certain why. There was nothing lacking in his physique; statistically he was the right height for his age, the right weight — well, perhaps a pound or two under (he detested the sight of food in any form before noon). Totally baffled, his physical education instructor, Mr. Tipton-Thomas, stood, hands on hips, shaking his head, looking the boy up and down. "Glick," he said, "I don't know what to think about you. You've got all the right parts: *two* arms, *two* legs, *two* eyes ... and only *one* head, thank God! But put 'em all together and they take off in seven directions at once."

The other kids in the gym class laughed, and Sandy Siltaanen, a popular blond blue-eyed kid and the best athlete in school, laughed hardest. "It's okay, Glick," said Sandy, catching his breath after another masterful jump, laying a big-brotherly arm around Max's drooping shoulders, "you got nothing to worry about. Someday you'll take over your dad's furniture business and guys like me'll end up driving your delivery trucks."

"Yeah? Who says so?" Selling china figurines to old ladies and kidney-shaped coffee tables to newlyweds was not Maximilian Glick's idea of a future.

Sandy Siltaanen, as cheerful about his dismal failures in the classroom as he was about his natural skill on the track or in the pool, smiled good-naturedly. "That's what my mom says every time I come home with another C-minus in history and a D in English."

Max wasn't sure what he detested most: was it that he was the gymnasium joke, the last choice whenever teams were chosen? Or that all his peers seemed to assume he would simply inherit the family furniture business someday and that would be that?

I have to become a Somebody, the boy lectured himself; a real Somebody. Look at Sandy — now *there* was a real Somebody: Sandy Siltaanen, who had walked, run, skipped, hopped, jumped, and dashed away with just about every trophy at the Northern Ontario Junior Olympics last fall; Siltaanen stepping onto the winner's podium on the final night of the games, his head a shining sheaf of wheat under the brilliant gym lights, those northern-blue eyes beaming out among the stalks, the shy-proud grin of victory, the applause, the shouts of praise and encouragement; Mr. Tipton-Thomas telling the *Steelton Star's* sports editor: "Rome ... Tokyo ... Stockholm ... the sky's the limit for a kid like that!"

There was a time when Maximilian longed to be known as the daring young Glick on the flying trapeze. Oh yes! To realize this dream, he compromised: with eyes closed, scarcely daring to breathe, he drank milk at breakfast, crunched his way through a terrible succession of cold cereals, even let the odd boiled egg slither down his throat; he did push-ups in the privacy of his room; at school he consciously adopted Sandy's stance — hands loosely on hips, head bent forward as if ready for flight. All to no avail.

His athletic ambition soon came to an abrupt end once and for all time on Parents' Night at school.

There it stood, the gym horse, raised to a height just challenging enough for an eleven-year-old. Any kid with enough coordination to step over a puddle could do it. A run of six or seven paces, then hit the springboard at the right spot, then somersault across the horse and onto the mat. One by one, led of course by the incomparable Siltaanen, the boys hurdled the horse, each successful somersaulter earning a burst of parental applause.

And then came Glick.

Maybe his run was too short. Maybe the spring in the springboard suddenly turned to molasses. Maybe the seemingly inert gym horse suddenly came alive and bucked like a bronco. All Max knew was that for a precarious moment he was sprawled on his stomach across the horse. His luck, like his arms and legs, seemed to have checked out without leaving a forwarding address. Over the side he tumbled, heavily, landing flat on his back like a dying cowboy. Mr. Tipton-Thomas ran from the sidelines and helped him to his feet. "Sorry folks," the gym teacher called to the audience, "somebody musta shot this fella's horse from under him."

Half-groggy, Maximilian glanced at the crowd in the stands. They were all laughing. He looked over at Henry and Sarah Glick. They too were laughing. His own father and mother . . . laughing.

"Well why not?" said Henry Glick later. "After all, it wasn't the end of the world. Anyway, Maxie, we weren't laughing *at* you, we were laughing *with* you."

"How could you be if *I* wasn't laughing?"

"Let's not get carried away with technicalities, Max," said Henry Glick, dismissing his son's embarrassment as if it were over nothing more earth-shattering than a ketchup stain on a new shirt. "Anyway, Max, athletics are like toys. They soon stop being important. At least, that's what *I* learned at your age."

Sarah Glick too refused to view the incident as anything more than a trivial mishap. "Maxie," she said, "you mustn't always take life so seriously."

"Why not?" Maximilian demanded. "*You* do. You're always worrying about what I'm going to be when I'm older."

"That's different, Maxie."

"How's it different?"

"We're your parents. That's what mothers and fathers are for . . . to worry. Now go soak those bones of yours in a nice hot bath."

A few days later, Maximilian sat at his desk in the small cheder, the Hebrew school, listening to Rabbi Kaminsky drum the history of Abraham and Abraham's descendants into his pupils' minds. "Abraham begat Isaac, who begat Jacob, who begat Joseph. . . ." At the conclusion of all these begats, the rabbi asked: "Now, who can tell me what those great figures had in common?"

Maximilian's hand went up first. "What they had in common," said Maximilian Glick, "was that Abraham worried about Isaac, who worried about Jacob, who worried about Joseph." The boy paused. "I don't remember who Joseph worried about."

After class, Rabbi Kaminsky took Maximilian aside. "I've heard some strange answers to that question over the years, but yours, Max . . . yours — "

The boy related the incident at the gymnasium on Parents' Night (which the rabbi, naturally, had already heard about) and his encounter with his parents after that calamity.

"They say I take life too seriously."

"That's a very serious accusation, Max. Are you guilty or not guilty?"

"I don't know." Max thought for a moment. "Guilty, I guess."

The rabbi now removed his gold-rimmed spectacles and set them down carefully on his desk. Slowly, gently, using thumb and forefinger, he rubbed his eyelids, his way always of summoning up some memory from his distant past. "How times change!" he said. "When I was your age, in our village in Poland, taking life *too* seriously was the only way we were allowed to take it. To study around the clock, to be pious, modest, respectful . . . these things were expected of us, even in our sleep. Fun? Fun was strictly rationed, like bread in a time of famine, like water in the desert. I remember once, Max, my worldly curiosity got the better of me, and I smuggled a newspaper from Warsaw into cheder. An ordinary harmless Jewish newspaper, Max! My teacher caught me reading it, and for that unpardonable frivolity I had to sit on a stool in the corner like a dunce for the rest of that week. 'The trouble with you, Kaminsky, is that you don't take life seriously!' I can still hear that old dragon scolding me; I can still see him waving his long pointer under my nose."

"How did you get out?" Maximilian asked.

"When I was sixteen my parents had to ship me off to Warsaw to further my Hebrew education. It was one of the happiest days of my life, that first day in Warsaw." The rabbi's eyes grew large, and he extended his arms wide, as if holding a ballooning world in the palms of his hands. "There was only one happier — the day I landed in Canada."

The rabbi put his spectacles back on and for a moment studied his pupil. "Tell me, Maximilian, why do you take life so seriously?"

"It's not my fault. It's theirs."

"Theirs?"

"My dad, my mom, my grandparents."

Rabbi Kaminsky's eyebrows shot up. "Really? How so? To me they always seem so high-spirited, like they all take from the same bowl of cherries."

"That's because you don't live with them," said Maximilian. "Sometimes I think they stay up all night thinking about nothing except how I'll get along when I'm thirty . . . will I eat a decent breakfast every morning . . . will I remember to tuck the shower curtain into the tub before I turn on the water."

Rabbi Kaminsky shook his head knowingly. "Times change. But some things remain the same."

"Did your parents drive you crazy?"

The rabbi, looking over his shoulder as if on the watch for spies, answered in a low voice. "The walls have ears, so I will tell you this quietly. *All* parents drive their children insane. Especially Jewish parents." He wagged a warning finger at Max. "Bear in mind," he said with mock severity, "if you ever quote me publicly, I will deny I ever made such a statement!"

"But why are Jewish parents worse?" asked Maximilian.

"It's not a matter of worse. It's a matter of different. Jewish parents don't really beget children, they *build* children. It's in our blood. It goes back through all the centuries when we had nothing else to build. You see, Max, you're not just a person, you're a piece of construction ... a building. And your parents are the building superintendents. If they keep checking the foundation, it's because — come rain, come wind, come earthquake — if you don't stand up, *they* don't stand up. Do you understand what I'm saying to you?"

Maximilian shook his head. He understood, but very little contentment flowed from this understanding. "I don't want to be a building," he said.

"Then what do you want?"

"To be a Somebody. So I can get out of Steelton ... like Sandy Siltaanen."

"You mean the Finnish kid that looks and moves like a Greek god?"

"Yes," said Max, surprised that the rabbi would know about the young athlete.

"May my sainted teacher forgive me, I read everything in the paper," explained the rabbi. "Even the Help Wanted ads."

Maximilian went on: "Our gym instructor says someday Sandy will be good enough to go to Rome and Tokyo and Stockholm ... places like that."

"But you, Max...." The rabbi smiled sympathetically. "You are not exactly a Greek god on your feet, are you?"

Max nodded sadly in agreement.

"Then you must find another way to be a Somebody, mustn't you?"

"But how?" There was a note of desperation in Max's question.

"The answer," said Rabbi Kaminsky, gazing intently at his pupil, "is right at your own fingertips. You want to get to Rome? To Tokyo? To Stockholm? Go home, Maximilian. Go home and practise!"

The boy took up his books and started out. At the door, he turned. "Mind if I ask you something, Rabbi?"

"'The timid cannot learn; the impatient cannot teach.' Ask."

"Why do you read the Help Wanted ads? Are you looking for another job?"

The rabbi laughed. "Maximilian, rabbis are not like Jerusalem. A rabbi can be here today" — he snapped his fingers — "and gone tomorrow."

"You mean," said Max, finding this incredible, "a rabbi can actually get fired?"

"Why not?"

"But you've been here all your life!"

"Max, there you go taking life too seriously again. Don't concern yourself, my friend. I plan to be here for the rest of my days, with a little luck. But I promise you, if there's a change in my plans, you'll be the first to know." The rabbi glanced at his gold pocketwatch. "Go home and practise," he commanded. "You've already wasted fifteen minutes. At this rate you'll never even make it to Warsaw."

Without another word, the boy was out the door.

At that moment Maximilian knew two things for certain — that he wanted Rabbi Kaminsky to be around forever and that he had *not* wasted fifteen minutes.

That Maximilian Glick hadn't wasted so much as a second of precious time was proven during his next piano lesson, when Derek Blackthorn suggested that Max should enter the annual Steelton Music Festival. "I think you're ready to compete at the Grade Eight piano level," said Mr. Blackthorn, chewing a mint — one of the many Max always made certain to bring with him, a defence against the tobacco-and-alcohol cloud that enveloped the grand piano and all who came within range.

Blackthorn glanced at a calendar on his desk. "The festival's scheduled for June fourth to ninth. About three months off." He flipped the pages of the festival syllabus. "Ah, here we are . . . Grade Eight Piano . . . let's see here . . . ah splendid, Max, splendid! They've set Mozart's Sonata Number Three in C-Major as the contest piece."

"Is that good?"

"It's not good, my boy," said Blackthorn, "it's *stupendous*! Listen — " And from memory Derek Blackthorn launched into the first movement. Before he'd played a dozen bars, Maximilian recognized the theme as one that had caught his attention before, probably on the radio.

When Blackthorn came to the end of the first movement, he punctuated the finale with a resounding C-major chord. "Well, Glick, as they say on Broadway, d'you think you can get in there and knock 'em dead?"

Max nodded an enthusiastic yes.

From Maximilian's package of mints Derek Blackthorn extracted two more. He gave one to his young pupil, and raised the other to eye level, just as Henry Glick had done with his wine glass on Max's eighth birthday. "To June fourth," he proclaimed, "and to victory!"

Teacher and pupil popped the mints into their mouths and for a moment or two chewed in silence.

At this point Shizuko Blackthorn, a ball of wet clay in hand, came in from her studio. "What's all the commotion?" she wanted to know. "I could hear the shouting all the way into my studio."

"Shizuko, my sweet," said her husband in an English accent that always reminded Max of newscasts on the BBC, "Maximilian Glick and I are toasting his forthcoming triumph at the music festival. Here, join us —" He handed her the package of mints.

For the first time since she and her English-born husband had met, Shizuko Blackthorn found herself drinking a toast by eating a mint.

4

It wasn't Carnegie Hall, but the auditorium of Steelton Collegiate Institute — "Steelton High" to the local populace — was the city's largest and used whenever some eminent personage, usually political, came to town. Indeed, over the years so many visiting politicians — including several prime ministers no less — had chosen this platform to cajole Steelton's voters during election campaigns that it had become known among local cynics as the "Stage of False Promises."

On occasion, however, true promise shone forth from that bare curtainless stage. A handful of budding artists — singers, pianists, violinists, trumpeters, clarinetists — had unfolded their talent and fortitude to audiences who loved music enough to brave the railway-station acoustics, a fickle ventilation system, and moulded plywood seats as unyielding as a country Baptist.

It was in this auditorium, five years earlier, that a slender sober girl whose house squatted in the shadow of the steel plant — Amy Czerczewski — seated herself at the only Steinway Grand in Steelton to take the long first step that would free her from the clutches of her bleak background. Her playing of Chopin's Ballade in G-Minor brought the audience, all eight hundred and fifty, to their feet, cheering and shouting "Encore!" In obedience to their demand, Amy Czerczewski then played the same composer's "Butterfly Etude," a performance so lambent one would have thought she herself was the winged creature. Only when the Steelton Concert Band rose in the orchestra pit and sounded the opening chord of the national anthem did the audience agree to let the young girl with the honey-colored braids leave the stage.

On this evening in June there were five contestants in the Grade Eight Piano category. Each had been given a number; the numbers were then drawn from a box, lottery-style.

The first, Bobby Rosenberg, was the son of Dr. Rosenberg, the local orthodontist. Dr. Rosenberg was determined that Bobby would not spend his life among faulty occlusions. No indeed, Bobby would be a concert pianist at all costs, even if it meant the good doctor was still fitting braces when he was ninety-five. There were just two problems: first, Bobby Rosenberg hated to practise. "Getting that boy to sit down at the piano is like pulling teeth," Dr. Rosenberg complained one night at the Glicks. Bryna Glick said: "That should be easy for you; after all, you *are* a dentist." Dr. Rosenberg, who never did extractions, didn't think this was funny and later that evening grumbled to Mrs. Rosenberg that old women like Bryna Glick should be seen but not heard.

The second problem was that Bobby Rosenberg had no talent. This fact he proceeded to demonstrate within the first twenty seconds of his performance.

Among the contestants waiting their turn anxiously in the wings were two festival officials, one of whom Maximilian heard whisper, "That kid plays like he's wearing gloves."

"Yeah," the other whispered back. "*Ski* gloves."

The second contestant was Frank Ianucci Jr. His father, Frank Ianucci Sr., was the proprietor of Frank Senior's Pizzeria and an amateur operatic tenor who knew exactly one song, "O Sole Mio," which he sang mostly at Italian weddings. Mr. Ianucci Sr. wanted Frank Jr. to be an orthodontist someday because, as everybody knew, orthodontists made a great deal of money — of which fact Frank Jr.'s mouth was proof. There was, Mr. Ianucci used to say, more metal in it than the steel plant produced in a day.

When Frank Ianucci Jr. finished his rendition of the sonata, everyone was convinced that the lad might be many things, maybe even an orthodontist — but a pianist? Never!

Next came Morton Kelly, a youngster whose nickname at Max's school was "Kelly-belly." At the moment Morton's problem — his stomach protruded and his arms were very short — made it difficult for him to maintain regular contact with the keyboard.

The same festival official who had whispered about gloves before, now said, loudly enough for Max to hear once again: "They oughta design a semi-circular piano for that kid, something that'll fit around him, like a life preserver."

After three disasters in a row, one of the festival officials commented to the other: "Well, so far, so bad. Who's next?"

There was a hushed pause in the auditorium while the adjudicator, Professor Lacoste, imported from the Toronto Conservatory of Music, penned a short memo in a looseleaf notebook. Then the portly professor gently touched a gong on his desk with a mallet, the signal for the next contestant to begin.

There was a moment of confusion in the wings.

"Number Four please —" the adjudicator called out.

Then two contestants started for the center of the stage at the same time. One was Maximilian Glick; the other a girl who'd been standing next to him in the wings biting her lip and taking deep gulps of air, looking every bit as pale and anxious as he.

"Well well," said the adjudicator, peering sternly over his reading glasses at the pair who had just walked to the Steinway, "what have we here, a duet? Perhaps it *does* take four hands to play this sonata properly after all."

"I'm Number Four sir," the young girl said timidly.

"I'm Number Four too," said Maximilian Glick.

"Congratulations," said the adjudicator. "You make a lovely couple and I hope you'll both be very happy." The audience broke into laughter and the adjudicator was very pleased with himself. "Now then you two," he said, "there seems to have been some mix-up. One must be Four and the other Five. Are the officials backstage?"

Looking sheepish, one of the officials emerged from the wings and positioned herself between Max and his fellow contestant. "I suggest you toss a coin," said the adjudicator to the official, "and whoever calls it correctly is Four. May the best man — or woman — win."

Again the audience laughed, and the adjudicator, thoroughly delighted at the way he was dealing with this crisis, rose and took a short bow.

But at center stage there was little or no amusement, as the official dug into her purse for a coin. "I hope I'm Four," the girl whispered to Max. "I just want to get this over with and go home."

"I hope I'm Five," Max whispered back. "I'm so scared I don't even think I could play the radio right now." Much of Max's self-confidence had evaporated as he'd watched contestants One, Two, and Three march on stage like seasoned professionals, only to slouch back into the wings at the conclusion of their performances.

After digging and fumbling in her purse, the official at last produced a penny which she held up in triumph. This time the audience applauded. "Heads or tails?" she asked Max and the girl.

"Ladies first," said Max.

"Heads," said the girl quickly.

"Tails." Max felt a little foolish. After all, what other choice did he have?

The coin shot up in the air, rolled over once on its way down, and disappeared down a hot-air vent in the floor a few feet from where the trio stood. While the festival official looked about embarrassed, laughter and applause rolled toward the stage from the crowded auditorium. The adjudicator, a man of surprising patience considering the musical horrors he had just seen and heard, rose from his seat, climbed to the stage, and addressed the audience. "When I was a postgraduate student of music at the Paris Conservatory," he explained, "I took a special course in coin-tossing. *Voilà!*" A twenty-five-cent piece rose high into the air and descended smartly into the palm of his hand.

"Tails," he announced, and looked to Maximilian. "Very well, Number Four. You may proceed." He smiled devilishly at the girl. "You, young lady, may retire to the wings to enjoy your reprieve." From the expressions on their faces, neither Max nor the girl was happy with the way Fate had dealt with them.

Max seated himself at the Steinway. In the audience his parents and grandparents stiffened in their seats. Across the aisle, Derek Blackthorn, looking as rumpled as ever in a dark brown corduroy suit, drew a fresh package of cigarettes from his jacket and began fidgeting nervously with the lid. Without doubt, if smoking had been permitted in the auditorium, Blackthorn would have smoked all twenty cigarettes at once.

The adjudicator nodded. The boy took a deep breath and felt his fingertips touch the cool ivory keys of the Steinway. Strange. He couldn't remember lowering his hands to the keyboard, but notes began to sound, whole strands and clusters of notes, some fast, some slow, some loud, some soft. He could feel the soles of his shoes on the pedals; he knew *something* was working down below, but had no idea how well or poorly. His right thumb and forefinger were certainly working to schedule, turning the pages of the music at precisely the right moment.

And then — suddenly — the big C-major chord. It was over. All over. And, just as suddenly, Maximilian Glick was standing center stage. There were applause, cheers, whistles from somewhere out there in the dimly lit hall full of faces.

And then he was back in the wings. Even here people were applauding. The two festival officials (including the lady with the penny) were smiling at each other, exchanging nods of approval. It finally dawned on Maximilian Glick that he had played well. Better than well. "Brilliantly!" That was the word the penny-lady used.

Again the hall fell silent. Again the gong sounded softly. Number Five made her way to the Steinway, seated herself and awaited the fateful nod. "Miss ... uh ... how's that pronounced?" asked the adjudicator, looking up at her.

"Brzjinski," the girl said meekly.

"I beg your pardon? —"

"Brrr-shin-skee," the girl replied, her voice fading.

"Hm," said the adjudicator, "it might help if you could insert a few more vowels between all those consonants."

This time the adjudicator's sense of humor brought forth a gale of laughter, while at the piano the young girl waited, her face now flushed. She swallowed hard, as if a watermelon had stuck in her throat and she were attempting to dislodge it. The gong sounded again.

After she had played, the audience greeted her rendition, as they had Maximilian's, with deafening cheers and applause. They would not laugh at the name "Brzjinski" again.

"This one will be a real horse race," Max heard one official say.

"I'm betting on Five," said the other.

"I'm betting on Four."

A third official suddenly appeared in the wings and poked her nose in. "It'll be a tie for sure," she said.

Professor Lacoste took hours — or so it seemed to Max — to finish writing out his comments in his notebook. At last he stood up to deliver his verdict. "Mozart's piano music," he began, "calls for a fine balance between delicacy and virility, gentleness and firmness. . . ." There followed a long-winded lecture about the proper technique for playing Mozart that Maximilian thought would never end.

Then, abruptly, the lecture was over, and so were the hopes of contestants One, Two, and Three. Professor Lacoste, summing up their attempts in a few words, smiled charitably over at them. "Let's just say they need . . . more work."

"Doing *what*?" whispered one of the officials behind Max.

Clearing his throat noisily, Professor Lacoste continued: "Now, we come to contestants Four and Five. . . ."

If someone had dropped a pin in the rear row, it would have resounded throughout the auditorium like rifleshot.

"I have been adjudicating at music festivals for over

twenty-five years," said Professor Lacoste. "This old back-
side of mine gets pretty numb sitting on a hard chair hour
after hour, these old ears of mine begin to ache a little after
several hours — or several days — of wrong notes, and these
old eyes grow dim and blurry. And then ... then ... every
once in a while ... praise be to God! ... along comes an
exception — like our young friend here, Miss Celia Brzjinski"
— this time he pronounced the name perfectly — "and life
seems again worthwhile."

One of the officials glanced at the girl in braids. "Another
Amy Czerczewski," she said.

Max told himself that this was it; Celia Brzjinski had won
the Grade Eight Piano prize.

Professor Lacoste went on to praise the girl's handling of
the piece. "A splendid, sensitive, surprisingly mature rendition!"

Another round of applause for Celia Brzjinski was cut short
when the adjudicator held up his hand for silence.

"Equally splendid, sensitive, and mature was the version
given to us by Mr. Maximilian Glick. If these two musicians
decide to enter the professional musical world some day, I
predict that Number Four will have problems with her second name, Number Five with his first name. Otherwise, these
two may well make a real name for themselves."

More laughter and applause.

"Lacoste should have been a stand-up comedian," said
one of the officials.

"I have decided in this instance to award the highest marks
I've ever awarded in this category because of the outstanding
musicianship displayed here." The professor's face now took
on a grave expression. "I have had to take into account one
special factor. One of the contestants handled the pedaling
with more taste, more discretion. The other was a bit heavy-
handed ... or should I say heavy-footed. And this is a crucial
consideration in a Mozart sonata. So...."

The adjudicator paused. Max stopped breathing. Celia
Brzjinski closed her eyes.

"So ... to Miss Celia Brzjinski I have awarded ninety-two marks —"

That was it. The girl had won.

"And to Mr. Maximilian Glick ... ninety-four."

A whoop sprang from somewhere in the audience. Max was certain it came from Bryna Glick. He'd heard something like it before, on the night of the Steelton Foods of the World contest, when Bryna's all-day spaghetti sauce edged out Mrs. Frank Ianucci's in the Italian category.

Maximilian was recalled to the center of the stage to receive his First Place Certificate. While he waited for Professor Lacoste to present it to him, he glanced out across the audience. With disbelief, he noticed Derek Blackthorn buttoning his jacket neatly and straightening his plain dark brown tie. Two miracles in one night!

5

On the drive home from Steelton High, Maximilian sat in the rear seat between the competing perfumes of his mother and grandmother, clutching the certificate rolled and tied with a gold ribbon. Henry Glick drove, while beside him Grandfather Glick gloated.

"The boy won by a mile," said Augustus.

"By a *foot*, is more like it," said his son.

Max's mother, overcome by the emotion of the night and a little weepy, spoke quietly. "I can't help feeling sorry for the girl."

"Nonsense," Bryna Glick snapped. "Max won fair and square. The girl was excellent. Maxie was more excellent. That's life. Somebody has to win, somebody has to lose."

"And you're the one that says what fun music is supposed to be," Sarah said.

"Of course it is, Sarah dear," replied Bryna. "The quest for excellence is always a thrill."

"Sounds awfully cold-blooded to me, Mother ... with all due respect."

From the front seat, Henry called over his shoulder: "C'mon you two, cut it out. This is Maximilian Glick's victory night."

Not another word was spoken, and Max could sit back, enjoying the respite, allowing his thoughts to rewind. For a moment he was on the stage again, blinded by the footlights, acknowledging applause from people he could barely see until, with some effort, he adjusted his vision to catch sight of Mr.

Blackthorn fingering the knot in his tie, just as the fastidious Rabbi Kaminsky would habitually pinch the knot in his whenever he rose to address his congregation.

Two men — Rabbi Kaminsky and Derek Blackthorn — as different as two men could be. The one with a military record now carrying himself in a stooped self-conscious posture, arms hanging long and awkwardly at his sides, as if all of him were strung together with baling wire; the other, having served in no militia in his life, but polished and straight as a sentry. Neither had ever said more than "Good day" to the other in passing, and yet both had become — each in his own way — Maximilian's personal luminaries, ascending to light his way and warm his youthful aspirations, descending long enough to let the boy be himself, all done with uncanny timing and reliability, like the rising and setting of the sun itself.

And Shizuko Blackthorn in her quiet unassuming way had also become part of Maximilian Glick's solar system. Though less than a second-rate housekeeper, she had become in Max's eyes a first-rate hostess. More and more often of late, Shizuko would invite Maximilian to stay after his lesson for tea, which she served from one of her delicately patterned ceramic teapots and which they drank out of small matching Japanese-style cups. It seemed to young Maximilian that at these simple tea-drinking sessions some entirely new and strange dimension in time was born. There was little talk of the past, the present, or the future. The three of them — the Blackthorns and Max — sat quietly, sipping, blowing through compressed lips to cool the steaming brew, sipping again. What conversation there was emerged softly, like the sound of the blowing and sipping, and concerned the changing but timeless colors of the St. Anne River, visible through the high old-fashioned bay window in the livingroom, or the equally timeless squealing of the seagulls forever scavenging along the river banks.

How different from the scene now in the Glick diningroom, where the family prepared to dig into Max's favorite cake — banana with orange icing. Sarah Glick had baked it that morning. If Max lost, the cake would be a consolation prize. If he won, it would add to the taste of triumph. As Max made his way through his second large slice, the family — that is, the older Glicks — began as always to talk about what lay ahead for their boy. Funny, thought Max, when it came to his comings and goings his parents and grandparents seemed to have eyes in the backs of their heads, and yet somehow their line of vision was always directed forward into the future — *his* in particular.

Eventually the tabletalk came round to another very special event due to take place in Max's young life — his bar mitzvah. After the summer holidays Max would begin a year of lessons and studies with Rabbi Kaminsky in preparation for his confirmation on his thirteenth birthday.

"You'll be a man at last," said his father Henry.

"He's a man now!" said old Augustus Glick. He turned to his grandson. "You've always been a man, haven't you, Maximilian?"

Even if Max's tongue hadn't been cemented in banana cake, the boy would have let his grandfather's question go unanswered. The whole business had grown ever so tiresome, the on-again–off-again manhood that constantly trailed Max like an uninvited pet, usually a few paces behind, sometimes drawing alongside, sometimes even a pace or two ahead. On the other hand, thought Maximilian, perhaps that was the price a person had to pay in the process of becoming a Somebody. Everybody — even Sandy Siltaanen — probably paid a heavy toll for the tonnage of expectations — his own as well as others'.

The following afternoon the front page of the *Steelton Daily Star* was taken up with an earthquake and flood in Bangladesh, a rebellion in Nicaragua, a subway strike in New York City, the sinking of an oil tanker off the coast of Spain. Sarah Glick glanced hastily over her husband's shoulder at the headlines. "Bad news and more bad news. Don't they ever print good news?"

Henry handed her the newspaper. "Open your eyes, Sarah."

"What? —"

"Look again —"

Sarah put on her reading glasses and squinted at the front page. "I don't see anything —"

"Look again," he laughed, pecking a finger into the lower right-hand corner of the front page, where, under a two-column headline that read "Highest Festival Mark To Pianist M. Glick," there was a photograph of Max (supplied to the press by the proud father himself, though he would deny it). The account spoke of "a breathtaking duel" between Max and Celia Brzjinski and quoted verbatim Professor Lacoste's glowing praise.

Not to be outdone, a television newscaster that evening called it "a local star war."

"Everybody's talking about it," Henry Glick exulted to his wife next day.

"Don't breathe a word to Maximilian," Sarah cautioned. "I don't want this thing to go to his head."

"Our son's a pretty solid citizen," Henry assured his wife. "Don't worry about it going to his head."

"Why not? It's already gone to *yours*."

Overnight Maximilian Glick had blossomed from a confused number in a list of contestants into a distinct piece of news. Thanks to fifteen minutes or so on the stage of Steelton High, he was no longer the kid who couldn't for the life of him tame a gymnasium horse; he was the kid who could take eight feet of piano and make it talk.

Such sudden fame would have been enough to take full possession of anybody's head, lock, stock, and barrel. In Max's case, however, that was impossible, for there was already a tenant occupying much of those premises. The tenant's name? — Celia Brzjinski.

Immediately after the near tie at the music festival, Celia's father made up his mind that his daughter should become a pupil of Derek Blackthorn. Mr. Brzjinski was convinced that the girl's former teacher, Miss Klemenhoog, was to blame for Celia's overpedaling which — slight though it was — had cost her a win in the Mozart. "Klemenhoog has big feet. No piano player should have such big feet," he declared. The fact that Derek Blackthorn pressed a pair of size twelves on the pedals was beside the point. "From now on, you'll take lessons from that Englishman," said Papa Brzjinski to his daughter. Of course Celia's mother brought up the matter of the Blackthorns' infamous style of living. "I'm a businessman," Mr. Brzjinski, a highly successful land developer, responded sharply. "I deal in financial statements. I look at the bottom line. If it's black, not red, I don't ask questions. Go call Blackthorn." And that was that.

It was inevitable that Celia and Maximilian should meet one day at the Blackthorns'. Their teacher lost no time. "Sit down you two," he ordered, pulling an extra chair up before the grand piano. On the music stand before them he plunked down a thick book with pages resembling battered parchment. "I used to play this four-hands arrangement with my Uncle Basil when I was a kid. He went on to become Sir Basil. I, alas, just went on. Better luck to you, Celia and Max. Now give it a try."

They played at sight the first few pages of Beethoven's Fifth Symphony, a transcription for four hands, while Blackthorn, using an unlit cigarette as a baton, conducted energetically and sang along in every vocal range from basso profundo to coloratura soprano. "Enough!" he called, part way through the movement. "My mind's made up. Next June you two will compete in the Four-Hands Open Class category."

"But that's for adults," said Celia.

"Of course," Blackthorn responded agreeably.

"We'll be up against people twice our age, maybe three times," Max pointed out.

"Then we shall simply have to accelerate your aging processes," Blackthorn proposed. "Leave you to dry out in the sun, the way they do with fish. Now then, no more of this stuff about who's adult and who isn't. Let's go back to bar twenty-four, please...."

Afterward Shizuko Blackthorn served tea. The four sat cross-legged around a low coffee table, its top scarred from cigarette burns and stained with rings left by countless damp drinking glasses. And yet to Maximilian the little tea ceremony suddenly acquired the miracle of elegance — the miracle was Celia Brzjinski. There was something about the way she brushed an errant strand of fair hair from her eyes; the way she held the handle-less Japanese teacup in her tapered fingers, as if it were a flower; the fact that she could sit cross-legged without hunching the way the girls on the volleyball team hunched during breaks. Above all, she could stay perfectly silent, while saying so much with the merest upturn of the corners of her mouth.

It turned out that the Brzjinskis lived just a few blocks from the Glicks, and Maximilian walked Celia home.

"What do you think of Blackthorn?" Max asked Celia after their lesson.

"I don't think he'd ever be any good at land development," answered Celia, recalling that the Blackthorn front yard was a living museum of weeds, "but in some ways he reminds me a lot of my father."

"How come?"

"They both say something can be done, and that's all there is to it. My father has this slogan framed over the desk in his office. 'A man's grasp must always exceed his reach.'"

"In that case," said Maximilian, "you know who should've won at the music festival?"

"Who?"

"Morton Kelly. His stomach exceeds his grasp, his reach, and everything else."

They walked past an old Anglican church with a small cemetery beside it. From the churchyard came the smells of freshly cut grass and of lilacs, their lavender blooms in contrast to the ivied stone of the church building and the uncompromising rectangles of gray and black granite that seemed to grow out of the tree-shaded ground.

"What do you suppose keeps people like the Blackthorns in a town like Steelton?" Maximilian asked.

"I don't know. Any time the subject comes up in our house,"

said Celia, "my folks automatically start talking Polish."

"Funny, mine start talking Jewish. You know Sandy Siltaanen?"

"Who *doesn't* know Sandy Siltaanen."

"His folks start talking Finnish."

"I guess that's what keeps foreign languages alive," said Celia.

The two continued at a leisurely pace, saying nothing until Celia broke the silence. "What's it like being Jewish?" she asked. "Is it true that all Jewish kids are born musical?"

Max pretended to be horrified. "That's gross! Who ever said they were?"

"My mother. The night you won at the music festival. My dad began to self-destruct on the way home, and said it was all Klemenhoog's fault ... you know, the thing about pedaling. But my mother said it was *your* fault."

"Fault?"

"Well, not really fault. What she said was, Jewish kids have an unfair advantage because they're born musical."

"You don't really believe that, do you?" asked Max.

Celia could tell he was trying not to laugh. "C'mon," she protested, "I'm very serious."

"Well, *do* you believe it, or *don't* you believe it?"

Celia thought about the question. "I don't know. There aren't any Jewish kids at the school I go to. You're the only one I've met."

"Remember Bobby Rosenberg?" Max asked.

"Who?"

"Bobby Rosenberg ... the first guy that played in our category?"

Celia grimaced. "He was a national disaster!"

"He was also a national *Jewish* disaster."

"Rosenberg's Jewish?"

Triumphant, Max nodded.

"You sure?"

"Sure I'm sure. Tell *that* to your mother."

There was a slight edge now to Max's voice, and Celia

began to regret that she'd brought up the subject. "I'm sorry," she said, "I hope I haven't said anything to insult you."

"It's okay. I just think you oughta set your mother straight, that's all."

"Easier said than done," said Celia. "Nobody argues with my folks. Once they make up their minds about something, that's it."

"Who's telling you to argue? Discuss."

Celia shook her head pessimistically. "All that stuff you hear on TV and radio about people communicating with each other ... well, the idea's never quite caught on in our family. If it's somebody's birthday you send them a card. If it's Christmas you give them a gift. If they're sick you keep out of their way and don't make any noise. Some nights it's so quiet at mealtimes you can hear people's watches ticking, especially if my dad's had a bad day at one of the construction sites. I sometimes think it's a miracle there's a piano in the house. My mother inherited it from her old Aunt Hattie. Three cheers for dear old Aunt Hattie!"

They resumed walking, still languorously. "You still haven't told me what it's like to be Jewish," Celia reminded Max.

"I'm not sure what to say. I mean, nobody's ever asked me that question before. I guess I'd have to say...." He broke off for a moment, thinking. "I guess I'd have to say in our case there's *too* much communication. Nobody ever shuts up. Everybody's got to put in their two cents' worth, you know? Also, if you're Jewish you worry an awful lot. You worry if you're not taking life serious enough, you worry if you're taking it too serious. And sometimes you say to yourself 'Hey, I'm not worrying about anything!' ... and then you *really* worry."

Warming to the subject, Max continued: "Also ... if there's one thing you need, it's a dynamite memory. Like ... you can't stuff a hunk of bubblegum into your mouth without remembering that somebody somewhere is starving. You can't tell a joke without being reminded that somebody's sick or dying. You can't look forward to anything without remembering something that happened way back in the past . . . usually bad."

Celia sighed. "Sometimes I wish I'd been born something else. Maybe it would've been different if my dad was Irish and my mother Polish, instead of the other way around. And maybe it wouldn't. Who knows? Do you ever wish you'd been born something else?"

"Uhuh. A Finn. I'd like to be a Finn, like Sandy Siltaanen."

"Why a Finn?"

"Because they're Scandinavians and all Scandinavians are natural athletes. That's a fact."

"How do you know that?"

"My dad," said Max. "He says it's in their blood."

Looking pensive, Celia slowed her step. "I don't understand something," she said. "If saying all Jewish kids are born musical is crazy, how come it's not crazy to say all Scandinavian kids are athletic?"

"Because my dad took all sorts of courses about people. At college. You know, philosophy, psychology, economics. He says, for instance, perfect strangers walk into his store and just like that" — Max snapped his fingers — "he can tell all about them . . . like how the inside of their house is decorated, what their cars are like, what they eat, even what they do for a living."

"Well," said Celia, "my mother was a nurse at Sacred Heart Hospital before she got married. She knows a lot about the human body. I'm going to check it with her."

"Check what?"

"If a Finn cuts himself and starts bleeding, do athletic corpuscles gush out all over the place?"

Max stopped in his tracks. He looked into Celia's face. No hint of an expression of any kind there. "You *are* putting me on?" Still no sign. He smiled shrewdly. "I think you just tied the score, right?"

"One gross idea deserves another." Celia smiled back.

"Okay, Brzjinski, we're even."

"Not quite. I'm still two marks behind you."

"That really bugs you, huh?"

"Yes."

"Relax," said Max, "If we do a number for four hands next year, we won't be competing against each other."

"So what," said Celia, teasing. "You'll still owe me those two points."

"Okay. Instead of calling ourselves 'Glick and Brzjinski,' we'll call ourselves 'Brzjinski and Glick.' Deal?"

Celia continued to play hard to get. "Well I figured we'd be called 'Brzjinski and Glick' in the first place. I mean, alphabetically or ladies first . . . no matter how you look at it, it should be 'Brzjinski and Glick.'"

"Maybe we oughta think about what Professor Lacoste said. Maybe I should change 'Maximilian' and you should change 'Brzjinski.'"

"Okay," Celia said, a little too agreeably, "I'll make *you* a deal, then. I'll change my second name to Jones . . . and you pick something nice and easy for your first name . . . like Tom, Dick, or Harry."

As they walked on, Max tested the new names thoughtfully. "Glick and Jones . . . Jones and Glick. . . . Not bad. Tom Glick? Dick Glick? . . . *Dick* Glick!"

"We stay with what we've got, then?"

"We stay with what we've got. That's final."

After a moment's reflection, Max said: "I think we oughta get ourselves a trademark."

"A trademark?"

"Like 'Chase and Sanborn.' So nobody can steal our name."

"How do you get a trademark?" Celia wondered.

"I don't know," Max replied. "I bet your dad's got one for his company. Why not ask him?"

"No thanks," Celia said. "All he'd say is: 'I never heard such a foolish idea.' Why don't you ask somebody in your family?"

"Are you kidding? Ask a question like that around our house and you immediately get three days of discussion. My family's like a closet full of wire hangers. Every time you reach for one, you get a whole armful, all tangled up."

"I vote we take our chances," said Celia. "Who'd want to steal a name like 'Brzjinski and Glick' anyway? Or 'Glick and Brzjinski'?" She laughed.

"You never know," said Max, very cautious and businesslike. "Especially if we become famous."

Celia frowned. *"If?"*

"Sorry. I meant *when.*"

Maximilian's sneakers carried him the rest of the way home, up Pine Hill, on columns of air. Once home, he decided not to go straight into the house where dinner was waiting, but flopped himself and his music books down on the steps of the front porch.

Below him lay the small city, ready — like himself — for summer. Of all the seasons, summer was the easiest to accept, the one that required little or no preparation; no snow shovels and salt to station beside the front steps, no wood to pile for the livingroom fireplace; no woolens to unpack. "Just summer," thought Max, "plain and simple. Here I am. Come and get me."

Heading into that summer, he could taste the sweet taste of Somebodyness. To get out of Steelton some day was still uppermost in his list of ambitions. But in the meantime there was July, there was August — there was Celia Brzjinski.

For the first time in his young memory, Maximilian Glick had the feeling that Steelton — from the steel plant on the western flank, to the ships' harbor on the eastern flank — Steelton was *his.*

6

It was the day after Labor Day that September. Liberated by a three-thirty bell he thought would never ring, Maximilian Glick took his place in the marathon that always had its starting line at the main school exit and its finish line a half-dozen blocks to the east, at Donut Heaven.

In the lead, as usual, was Morton Kelly whose legs, at times like this, moved with remarkable swiftness considering they supported twice the weight God intended. Morton's mid-section reminded Maximilian of the earth's equator, a bloated circumference barreling headlong through the streets toward that mystical ring of fried dough that would keep him alive until six o'clock when Mrs. Morton uttered his favorite sound: Supper!

Well behind him followed Maximilian, in company with Duncan Sargent ("Sarge" to everybody) who lived a few doors away. The two were engaged in a contest to determine who could list the greater number of detestable things about the first day back at school.

"The smell of varnish, fresh paint ... and floorwax," said Sarge.

"The smell of wool sweaters," said Maximilian, referring to pullovers freed from dozens of musty closets and chests. "Also Mr. Hussey's after-shave lotion and Miss Irvine's perfume."

"You got it all wrong, Glick," said Sarge. "*He* uses perfume; *she* uses after-shave. You ever take a look at what's over her upper lip?"

They continued with the list, each new item eliciting heart-felt groans of distaste.

"My older sister started Latin today," Sarge said. "I can tell already I'm really gonna hate Latin."

"Who speaks Latin anyway?"

Sarge, whose father owned a pharmacy, said: "Funny you should ask. My dad does. You gotta know Latin to run a drug-store."

"How come?"

"I dunno. So you can talk to your customers, I guess."

There was a momentary lull. "Know what depresses me?" Sarge frowned. "History. People really did boring stuff, like cutting off this king's head and that king's head. We got Old Stoneface Stone this year for history. She says anybody that ignores history is doomed to repeat it. I wonder what *that's* supposed to mean."

"It means if you don't pay attention you have to take the same course all over again next year."

Sarge shook his head woefully, as if sentence had already been passed.

"Know what depresses me?" Max said. "All those phony teachers' smiles on opening day. You watch ... tomorrow morning every single one of 'em will show up with horns and fangs."

Sarge agreed wholeheartedly. "And covered with slimy green scales," he added, cringing as if he were about to be brushed by one of the hideous teaching-monsters.

"All except Miss Creley," Maximilian said.

"Who's Miss Creley?"

"Our new math teacher. She's really something!" Max whistled softly.

"Is she the one with the real bright purple dress?"

"Oh you noticed, huh?"

"Noticed! You gotta be blind not to notice."

"Know what she did?" Max asked. "She climbed up on her desk, see? ..." Max stopped in his tracks to demonstrate. "And she stands there with her hands down at her sides, tight, like this ... and her legs apart, like this. 'Know what this is?' she says. 'It's an isosceles triangle.' And Frank Ianucci, who's sitting in the front seat right in front of her desk, says, 'Gee, Miss Creley, I thought it was a slice of pizza.' Everybody laughs, and Miss Creley says, 'Okay Frank, for showing off you stay half an hour after class.' And Rosenberg puts up his hand and says, 'Miss Creley can I stay instead 'cause Frank's gotta go to his grandmother's funeral as soon as school's over?' So Creley gives Rosenberg a detention too. By the time she's finished showing us what an isosceles triangle looks like, eight guys in the class have detentions. *I* would've tried to get a detention except I gotta be at my Hebrew class sharp at four."

"Hebrew! What're you gonna do with Hebrew?" Sarge asked.

"Same thing as I'm gonna do with Latin. Be a shepherd. S'long. See you tomorrow, Sarge."

Breaking ranks, Maximilian took off now in the direction of Rabbi Kaminsky's house. He carried an armload of textbooks the rabbi had prescribed a few days earlier for his bar mitzvah course. With cheder suspended during the summer months, the boy hadn't seen much of the rabbi and he looked forward to this, his second private lesson, especially since the first had come with what Mrs. Kaminsky called "a bonus."

Like Mrs. Blackthorn, Mrs. Kaminsky served tea whenever pupils came for private lessons in her husband's tiny study. The ritual here, though as pleasant as at the Blackthorns', was a far different affair. Water was heated in a silver samovar brought all the way from Mrs. Kaminsky's childhood home in Rumania. The samovar sat on a heavy silver tray, which in turn rested on an immaculate white cloth that protected the polished top of the mahogany sideboard. To Max these objects — the samovar, tray, cloth, dark sideboard — seemed to be part of each other, as if assembled and maintained not simply for tea, but to keep something alive — something that existed ages ago and thousands of miles away, something about which a boy, born and raised in a northern city in Ontario, could have only a vague comprehension.

Rabbi Kaminsky drank his tea steaming hot from a thick glass which he held at the rim almost daintily, between thumb and middle finger, his index finger cocked stylishly high. He strained the strong black tea through a lump of sugar balanced deftly on his tongue. There was fresh spongecake and poppyseed cookies. The conversation was animated. It seemed as though teatime in the quiet Kaminsky household was when one's thoughts — bottled up since morning — were suddenly uncorked and permitted to pour generously across the happenings of the day — the wars, the weather, anything and everything. Bits of gentle gossip filled the spaces between world news — whose house needed painting, whose car had been de-fendered during a particularly unruly few minutes at the corner of King and Queen, who was threatening to take whom to court because of it.

But to Maximilian the wonderful thing about the Kaminskys was that — unlike so many people of their generation — they were as adept at the art of listening as they were at the art of talking. It seemed to Maximilian that whenever groups of adults got together for whatever reason, everyone spoke at once, whether it was friends bantering or exchanging family news bulletins, or adversaries playing king-of-the-castle over some controversy — usually involving the management of the synagogue. But the rabbi and his wife, seldom if ever interrupting each other, spoke in a measured way, strolling through a topic as if on a Sunday walk and stopping every few paces to listen.

One thing about the Kaminskys, however, had puzzled Maximilian. "How come the Kaminskys never had any kids?" he asked his parents, after his first private lesson.

Henry and Sarah Glick exchanged hasty glances, but neither volunteered a reply.

"How come they never had kids?" Max said, looking first to one, then the other.

Henry coughed into his napkin.

"Well," said Sarah slowly, "they had . . . I mean they have . . . a child . . . a daughter —"

"They *do*?"

"Yes. Eat your dinner, Maxie, it's getting cold."

"Where is she?"

"She's away," Sarah replied casually, shrugging her shoulders in the hope that a show of indifference would end the inquiry.

"Away? Where?"

"I don't know, Max. I think in the States someplace."

"How come nobody ever talks about her? I didn't see any pictures of a kid on their walls, like we have all over this place."

"That's because your mother and I have this hang-up, Maxie." Henry chuckled, hoping he'd managed to sidetrack his son's questions for the night.

"I'm serious," Max protested.

"Yes I know you are, Max. Much too serious. Your fish'll be like ice in a moment. Eat."

"You know I can't stand fish."

"That's fresh whitefish ... straight from Lake Superior," said Sarah. "Caught this morning."

"Great," said Max. "Tell 'em to go back and catch the rest of it. All they caught was the bones. Where is Rabbi Kaminsky's daughter and how come they never talk about her?"

"If we tell you, will you finish your fish?" asked Henry.

"No," said Maximilian bluntly.

"Waste not, want not." Henry Glick leaned across the table and forked Maximilian's uneaten fish on to his own plate.

Not content with partial victory, the boy pressed his inquiry. "Is somebody going to tell me about Kaminsky's daughter? Is she a Russian spy or something?"

Sarah Glick sighed with resignation. "Maxie, the reason nobody mentions Rita Kaminsky is because ... well, it's because many years ago ... before you were born ... while she was at teachers' college in Nickel City, she met this young man ... he was also at teachers' college ... and— uh — they got married to each other —" She hesitated.

"What's so terrible about that?" Max said. "You and Dad met at college and got married to each other."

"Yes, but it wasn't quite the same. The man Rita married
. . . well, he wasn't Jewish, you see."

"What was he?"

"Oh God," Sarah said in exasperation, "you really should
be a district attorney when you grow up, Maxie. How you
cross-examine!"

"I don't understand," said Max. "What was the man?"

Equally exasperated, Henry Glick blurted out: "He was
purple with green spots."

"You mean anybody who's not Jewish is purple with green
spots?"

"Exactly!" cried Henry Glick. "There are two kinds of people
on this earth: Jews and people who are purple with green
spots." He turned to his wife. "Sarah, for godsake what's for
dessert?"

"Fresh pineapple," Sarah replied.

"Straight from Lake Superior . . . caught this morning,"
said Max.

"Don't be a smart alec, young man," Henry said.

"Then tell me what was wrong with the man Rita Kaminsky
married. Was *he* a Russian spy?"

"I've told you what was wrong: he wasn't Jewish," Sarah
Glick said. She rose from the table. "I'll get dessert."

"What? You're leaving me here alone . . . with *him*?" Henry
shouted at his wife.

Sarah Glick sat down again. "Maxie," she said, looking
intently into the boy's face, "you're a bit young to understand. . . ."

There it was again, thought Maximilian, the on-again–off-
again manhood. At this particular moment it was apparently
off. "I want to know," he said.

"I repeat, Maxie, you're a bit young, but I'll try to explain
the situation. Rita Kaminsky married a Gentile, a man not of
the Jewish faith. Her parents, being very religious, very traditional, were naturally greatly upset, so upset in fact that they
observed a week of mourning . . . shiva, it's called in Hebrew
. . . as if their daughter had died. There's been no communi-

cation between the Kaminskys and Rita ever since, as far as we know. They never mention her name, and we've learned never to ask about her. The whole subject is extremely painful to the Kaminskys, especially since Rita was an only child."

"What did they do during shiva ... tear their clothes like people did in the Bible?"

"No, Maxie. Despite their grief, Rabbi Kaminsky is not a clothes-tearer. They simply stayed indoors at home, draped all the mirrors in the house with sheets, said special prayers ... things of that sort."

"But she was still alive. I don't get it."

Henry Glick spelled his wife at this point. "Max, a great many Jews, in fact most Jews, regard intermarriage ... that is, marriage between a Jew and a Gentile ... as if it's a ... well, I suppose sin is the best word. To Rabbi Kaminsky and his wife, their daughter had committed a sin, an unpardonable one at that."

Maximilian frowned. "That doesn't make sense. Rabbi Kaminsky told us at cheder that one of the things that makes people different from animals is that people commit sins; the other thing that makes people different is that they forgive sins."

"There's an old saying: To err is human, to forgive divine. But one of the things that also makes people different from animals is that we don't always practise what we preach, not even when we are rabbis and teachers. And I guess Rabbi Kaminsky couldn't find it in his heart to forgive his daughter. Simple as that."

But to Maximilian it wasn't as simple as that, not at all. "Why is intermarriage a sin? Why is it so terrible?"

Now it was Sarah Glick's turn to take the helm. "Your dad and I aren't necessarily saying it's a sin, or that it's terrible. Those are pretty strong terms —"

"Then why do most Jews think so?"

"Because — uh —" Sarah shot a look across the dinnertable at her husband, a plea for emergency assistance.

"Because we feel that intermarriage weakens our traditional values, our — uh — cultural heritage. It dilutes us as a people ... yes, dilutes is a good word." Henry Glick sat back in his chair, satisfied with his choice.

"I thought 'dilute' is when you add water to something. Is that what happens when you marry a Gentile ... you add water to the Jews?"

"Yes," Henry Glick replied.

"What's the difference between how Rabbi Kaminsky feels about Rita marrying a Gentile, and race prejudice?"

Henry asked: "Who's been talking to you about race prejudice?"

"Our teacher, at school. What's the difference?"

Henry took a moment to reflect. "I would say ..." he said slowly, "that race prejudice is a negative thing. I mean, its purpose is to put down a certain race. But being against inter-marriage is a positive thing. We are proud of our faith, our customs, our language. We want to see these things preserved, you see. Otherwise, we Jews are liable to disappear off the face of the earth." Max's father paused to let this sink in. "Do you understand what I'm saying, Max?"

"If I ever marry a Gentile, will you go into mourning as if I was dead?"

"You refuse to eat broiled whitefish once more and I may treat you as if you're dead, young man," said Sarah Glick. She rose from the table again, this time with an air of determination. Nothing was going to stop her from serving dessert. At the same time Henry Glick reached for the evening paper which he liked to read over coffee and a cigarette, despite the fact that he knew his wife eyed every puff of smoke with hostility as it curled upward into the chandelier and dissipated among the crystal teardrops.

Maximilian understood these signs. They meant that the conversation had come to an end, at least for the time being. There was a hint of exhaustion in the way his father settled back in his armchair, the upper part of him hidden now behind the open newspaper. His mother's shoulders seemed to sag a little too, and she took a deep breath as she made her way through the swinging door into the kitchen to fetch the coffee pot. In the boy's mind there were still questions, and questions *within* questions, simmering like Bryna Glick's famous all-day spaghetti sauce. But the answers would clearly not come this night. One day soon, Maximilian told himself, he would bring up the matter again with his mother and father. Better still, he would wait for the right moment and ask Rabbi Kaminsky himself. None of the answers he'd received over dinner had laid his curiosity to rest. "The timid cannot learn ... the impatient cannot teach...." Yes, he would wait for the right moment, and he would ask Rabbi Kaminsky himself.

The boy glanced at his wristwatch. Four o'clock. He was right on time. He knocked on the front door. There was no answer. He knocked again, this time a bit louder. From inside he could hear voices. Once more he knocked, rapping the door sharply. Still no reply. Setting his books down on the stoop, he tried the door. It was unlocked. Hesitantly he opened it.

"Oh Max, it's you, dear —"

To his astonishment the person greeting him was Bryna Glick. Behind her were Sarah, Augustus, Henry. In fact, the boy realized instantly that the Kaminsky house was filled with people. It seemed that just about the entire Steelton Jewish community was gathered in the house for some reason. Then he caught sight of Mrs. Kaminsky, seated on the chesterfield in the livingroom, between friends who held her hands, rubbing them gently, consoling her. The old woman rocked to and fro and from side to side, eyes half-closed, mouth slack. In the hallway, a large mirror had been draped with a sheet, as had another mirror over the sideboard in the diningroom. "What's wrong, did Rita Kaminsky die again?" Max said to his grandmother.

Stunned by the question, Bryna Glick turned to her daughter-in-law. "What on earth is he talking about, Sarah?"

It's all right Mother," Sarah replied. She took her son's hand and led him toward the door. "Maxie, there will be no lesson today...." Sarah Glick's voice broke; she cleared her throat but for a moment or two the words would not come. Her eyes, dry up to this point, became a blur behind tears.

"It's Rabbi Kaminsky, isn't it?" Max said.

Sarah nodded.

"He's dead —"

"Yes."

"What happened?"

"A bus ... the one that takes passengers to the airport ... he was crossing the street ... against a red light —"

From the livingroom Mrs. Kaminsky's voice was heard for the first time. "I told him a million times ... a *million* times ... never cross when a light's red. He wouldn't listen —"

Maximilian recalled the rabbi's confident stride, more like a march most of the time, heels smacking the sidewalk, the sharp creases of his trousers cutting a path for him through the strongest wind.

"Is it okay if I stay?" asked Max.

"No, Maxie, there are no other children here. I think it's best if you go on home. We'll be along soon."

"But —"

"Maxie, dear," Sarah cut in firmly, "this is not the time or the place for children."

"I'll never see him again, will I?"

"No, Maxie. But tomorrow, you can come to the station." There being no Jewish cemetery in Steelton or Nickel City, after the funeral it was necessary to transport the rabbi's remains to Toronto.

On the following afternoon the platform at the railway station — usually bare except for a few railway employees and a handful of passengers bound for Toronto on the 4:10 — was crowded. Everyone in the Jewish community, including several mothers with babes in arms, had turned up at the station to bid farewell to Rabbi Kaminsky. His coffin had been loaded carefully into a freight car earlier, and now Mrs. Kaminsky, with two of her closest friends going along for company, was boarding a passenger car for the sad voyage.

"Board!" called the conductor. With the sound of steel

crunching and grinding against steel, the train lurched forward unsteadily, as if it understood its role in this sorrowful scene.

Max watched the cars pass before him. For a second or two it seemed as if he and the platform under his feet were moving and the cars standing still. He looked about him. People were waving, some weeping quietly. Augustus Glick was dabbing his old eyes with a handkerchief that was gray with dampness. Bryna Glick's eyes were hidden behind sunglasses. Sarah and Henry Glick too hid their eyes behind sunglasses. There was Morris Moskover, the Local Sage, silent for one of the rare moments in his life.

And then Maximilian's attention was drawn beyond the inner circle of Jews, to another large gathering of men and women who had come to the station and now stood looking mournful as the last car in the train rounded a bend beyond the station and disappeared heading eastward. The people in the inner circle presented no surprise to Maximilian. But the people in the outer circle, standing about a bit awkwardly and shaking hands with the rabbi's congregants . . . *they* were a surprise to the boy.

They were the purple people, the ones with the green spots.

Part Two

7

It is no exaggeration to say that the young rabbi hired to replace Rabbi Kaminsky became the talk of the town within twenty-four hours of his setting foot in Steelton.

With the approach of Jewish high holidays in October — Rosh Hashanah, the New Year, and Yom Kippur, the Day of Atonement — it had been urgent that a new rabbi be found, and the Central Jewish Agency in Toronto, charged with the search, dispatched a report in record time to Zelig Peikes, president of Steelton's Jewish community: "We believe we have just the right man. He's young, a bachelor, native of Boston. . . ." The agency then listed all the colleges, seminaries, and special courses the rabbi had attended. "The man's got more degrees than a thermometer," Peikes reported to his executive. "Perfect," said Harry Zwicker, the secretary. "Call in the order and request immediate delivery."

"Mr. Zwicker," said the president officiously, "we know you run a tobacco shop, but a rabbi is not a carton of cigarettes!" Zelig Peikes, an old-fashioned man, liked to observe certain formalities. He therefore sent a telegram to the Agency in Toronto: "Steelton Jewish Community hereby signifies approval of party recommended as its spiritual leader. Stop. Early arrival of said party important to continuing congregational religious functions. Stop. Please acknowledge." The telegram had come to $11.60, and Milt Katzenberg, the treasurer, reminded the president that the message could have been sent using half the words. "The trouble with you, Mr.

Katzenberg," Zelig Peikes responded with the haughtiness of his office, "is that you have no sense of what looks good in official circles."

The moment the new rabbi stepped off the airport bus (the same that had dispatched poor Rabbi Kaminsky) everyone on the executive committee — Peikes, Zwicker, Katzenberg — wished they'd moved a bit more slowly. In fact, they didn't at first first *believe* the sight that stood before them.

The young man (he was thirty-one) wore a wide-brimmed black hat so large that his face was scarcely noticeable. A black frock coat with black satin lapels reached well below his knees, reminding the welcoming committee of a bathrobe from some previous century. A black string tie hung limply from his white shirtcollar. His feet, too long and too broad for so short a person, were encased in a pair of well-brushed black shoes, and white socks blinding in the midst of so much black.

"My God," whispered Harry Zwicker.

"Next time the *Agency* can pay for the telegram," whispered Milt Katzenberg.

The new rabbi, it turned out, was a member of the Lubavitcher sect, an extremely Orthodox group who clothe themselves in the fashion of their Eastern European forefathers and wear their beards long, their sideburns untrimmed.

"Gentlemen, gentlemen, a little decorum please!" said Zelig Peikes out of the side of his mouth. He stepped forward and offered his hand. "Welcome to Steelton, Rabbi Teitelman — "

The new rabbi managed a weak smile. "I'm afraid I'm not a very good flyer. Is there a. . . ." He hesitated, glanced in the direction of the bus depot, then fled.

"Marvelous. Wonderful," said Zwicker, while the committee waited outside. "We ask for a rabbi, and they send us a walking sideshow . . . a black angel that can't fly."

"Have faith," said Milt Katzenberg. "God giveth, God taketh away. When it comes time for God to take him away from us, we'll do him a favor and buy him a train ticket."

Zelig Peikes, president of the congregation, said nothing.

But the presidency meant a great deal to him. This was his fourth term in office, and he wondered whether the hiring of a Lubavitcher rabbi (of all things!) might cost him a fifth.

Peikes's concern was well-founded, for the shock of meeting the new rabbi was almost too much for the local community, both Jewish and non-Jewish. Never had the towns-people seen anyone outfitted in such a costume, even at the annual Mardi Gras run by the local branch of the Sons of the Holy Society of St. Christopher. Never had the shop windows on the main streets, which the young rabbi passed on his walks, reflected so pale a countenance. Never had the barbers downtown, whose scissors had shorn everything from tearful two-year-olds to lumberjacks fresh from the woods and with a full winter's growth, seen such long curly sidelocks, such red hair. Whenever the young Lubavitcher rabbi took to the streets for a breath of air, passing motorists slowed their cars to gawk, children stopped their games to look, merchants and customers halted trade to stare.

Before too many days had passed, the Lubavitcher rabbi — unassuming, unaware, without the slightest intention — had managed to capture the attention of the entire city, much the way a visiting magician or seller of elixirs might have done in horse-and-buggy times.

Minor miracles were attributed to him.

A bank manager claimed that a suspicious-looking pair of strangers, whom he took for bank robbers, turned and fled unnerved when the black-clad clergyman happened to enter the bank merely to cash his paycheck. Then there was the time when the rabbi, visiting Mrs. Moskover in hospital, bent to scratch his ankle, noticed a loose connection in the adjoining patient's oxygen line, and alerted a nurse just as the unfortunate man in the plastic tent was turning blue.

Morris Moskover, the Local Sage, also at his wife's bedside at the time, took a secular view of the incident. "It's very simple," said Moskover. "The rabbi had an itch to do good." But to Father Darcy, the dour chaplain of Sacred Heart, the hand that scratched the ankle was no less than the benevolent hand of God.

And finally there was the day in mid-October when the maple trees in Steelton and the surrounding countryside were at the peak of their autumnal flame, the day before the Day of Atonement. The rabbi had led a handful of the more observant Jews to the banks of the St. Anne River, there to conduct the ancient symbolic rite of jettisoning one's sins by emptying one's pockets into the water. Unfortunately, the town's poorest Jew, Nathan Pripchik, in turning out his trouser pockets, inadvertently deposited his last ten-dollar bill into the river where it was quickly caught in the steady current and began drifting toward a stretch of rapids. Without hesitation the new rabbi leapt into the chilly water, soaking himself to his middle, and retrieved the bill for poor Pripchik.

All the next day the Lubavitcher rabbi heroically led the congregation in its holiest of holy day worship, chanting fervently in his high-pitched nasal tenor, bending his body to and fro in the traditional choreography of Hebrew prayer, alternately perspiring and shivering with a high fever. Still, because of the rule of fasting that governed the Day of Atonement, he resolutely refused water or medication. At sundown, after managing to blow the final blast on a ram's horn to signal the end of worship, Rabbi Teitelman collapsed, but not before hearing gasps of awe and admiration from many of his flock.

The young Lubavitcher rabbi in old-country garb and reddish sidelocks may not have been what the Jewish congregation had bargained for. The exact opposite of Rabbi Kaminsky in so many ways, he was generally serious and reserved. Nevertheless, as Bryna Glick put it after breaking her fast, "The corporal suddenly became a captain!"

Something else happened that the Jews of Steelton hadn't bargained for. The new rabbi's presence had now aroused the city's inquisitiveness about its Jewish population, an inquisitiveness that had slumbered beneath cobwebs — with everyone's blessing — for years.

The current generation of Jews, many of whom stood behind the very counters where their fathers had done business, or in the very kitchens where their mothers had baked loaves of challah for the Sabbath, lived unobtrusive lives. If Steelton were compared to a house, the foundation stones would be Anglo-Saxon, the bricks French, the mortar Italian, Slav, and Scandinavian. The small community of Jews was hinged to the structure like a window shutter, with the light passing right through. Most of the townspeople knew the Jews were there, knew that they paid their taxes, voted on election days, helped sponsor the local amateur hockey team, bought apples from the Boy Scouts and cookies from the Brownies, entered their kids in the music festival. But beyond those civic activities, what?

Suddenly, unexpectedly, there was an air of curiosity, and the Jewish community felt itself magnified, trapped under a gigantic microscope, scrutinized day and night. Out of the blue, neighbors who had formerly minded their own business or simply been indifferent were asking polite but pointed questions.

Suddenly, the Jews of Steelton felt accountable.

Amos Kerkorian, a corner grocer still popular with many of the old-time Jews, wondered how the young rabbi managed to exist on such a restricted diet. "The old rabbi used to buy all sorts of things here," he said " — fish, cheese, breakfast cereal, frozen juice, even chocolate and candies once in a while. But this new fella, all he ever buys is eggs and more eggs, and a little fresh fruit and vegetables, just about enough to feed a bird. And nothing, absolutely nothing else. Beats me."

"It's because we have strict laws about food," Sarah Glick, one of Mr. Kerkorian's regular customers, reminded him. "It's called 'keeping kosher.'"

"Yes, yes, I know all about that," Kerkorian said, "but how is it that so many of you are steady patrons of Hong Ling's China Palace?" Hong Ling's was the best of several Chinese restaurants in Steelton. On Sunday nights especially, local Occidentals — many of them Jews — lined up to eat home-made Oriental dishes — sweet-and-sour shrimp, egg rolls, chow mein — foods Sarah Glick's Orthodox ancestors in Eastern Europe wouldn't have touched with a ten-foot chopstick.

"Well," said Sarah Glick, pretending to be indignant, "you don't expect us to eat at the place next door, do you?" She was referring to a fried-chicken franchise operation, a gaudy red and white shop that exhaled an overwhelming odor of burning french fries around the clock. "After all," she added "we Jews *invented* chicken."

When Maximilian Glick's mother related this conversation to her circle of friends at the synagogue Ladies' Auxiliary, no one but she saw the humor in it. From that time on, Hong Ling's Jewish customers made a practice of avoiding Sunday nights at the Chinese restaurant. And even on other nights of the week, when the arborite tables and padded vinyl booths were otherwise empty, the Jews huddled over their platters of barbecued spareribs self-consciously, as if all eyes — including the eyes of their Cantonese host — were upon them.

The manager of the hardware store next to A. Glick & Son, Cal Irwin, over morning coffee and donuts in the nearby bakery, wondered aloud why, for the first time in his memory (which went back many years), so many Jewish shops were closed on Saturday mornings. "I guess the rumor's true, eh Henry?" Cal Irwin said to Henry Glick.

"What rumor, Cal?"

"That you're goin' to Sabbath services 'cause Ol' Redbeard has put the fear of the Lord into you folks. And here I thought the only person in the world you were afraid of was your wife."

Determined to be a good sport, Henry Glick laughed. Inwardly, however, it was a different story. For the first time in Henry Glick's memory (which also went back many years) he was beginning to feel like a sore thumb.

Minor tremors of discontent began to rumble through the small Jewish community. Unfortunately the rabbi, still unaware, did nothing to diminish them.

To make matters worse, there was the sermon he chose to preach for some unexplained reason during Chanukah — a festival of good cheer and gift-giving that fell early that December. Rabbi Kaminsky would have recited a passage of scripture, a psalm or two, and led the audience in singing Hebrew songs of rejoicing in his resolute baritone. Rabbi Teitelman, however, took the occasion to deliver a fiery message about — of all things — Evil. The dais from which he spoke, at the center of the modest sanctuary, was raised from the floor by only two or three steps. But the Lubavitcher's words cascaded down upon his listeners like a magistrate's verdict. Vanity, Greed, Lust, Hypocrisy — all these human failings were spread before them like a catalogue of sins, inviting admissions of guilt.

"Was he talking about *us*?" old Augustus Glick asked afterward, his disbelief bordering on outrage.

Zelig Peikes was reassuring. "Relax, Mr. Glick. He was really talking about the congregation in Nickel City."

But Augustus Glick was not reassured. "Zelig, my friend," he said in a fatherly tone, "you *do* want to be president of this congregation for a fifth term, don't you?" Peikes said nothing, but the words "I do, I do!" hovered around his lips as if he were an eager groom at a wedding. "Then Zelig my friend," said the old man, "go to Rabbi Teitelman and tell him — in a nice way, mind you — that he's got a lot to learn."

Others nodded in solemn agreement.

A few days later Peikes met with the young Lubavitcher rabbi.

"Rabbi," he began slowly, deferentially, "we appreciate that you are reviving customs and reminding us of certain obligations that have ... shall we say ... gone by the way over the years. But do you think you are making life any easier for us Jews?"

"Since when has life ever been easy for Jews?" asked the rabbi.

Peikes gave the rabbi's reply a moment's thought. "Rabbi, I know you mean well, but do you think our people will be satisfied with such an answer?"

The rabbi too paused to reflect. Then he smiled. "When have our people ever been satisfied with answers?"

Always a question answered by a question — this was an old-fashioned form of debate among Jews. Peikes knew he must alter the pattern of dialogue between the rabbi and himself; otherwise he would return to Augustus Glick and his supporters empty-handed. "I hope you will forgive a direct statement. Rabbi Kaminsky, may he rest in peace, was a devout Jew like yourself. But he made allowances. What I mean is ... there were certain realities of life here that he understood."

"I was never fortunate enough to know my predecessor," replied the new rabbi, "but the reason he rests in peace is that he did not understand *every* reality. Like the rules of traffic, for instance." The rabbi shrugged. "But then, who does?"

Zelig Peikes returned to his followers. "Well Peikes," they demanded, "what news?"

Gloom darkening his face, Peikes extended his hands toward them, palms up, empty.

And so the discontent festered and grew, and the Jewish congregation became less and less happy by the day with their young rabbi, with his effect on Steelton and on their lives.

But no one among them was less happy with the Lubavitcher rabbi than his new pupil — Maximilian Glick.

8

Maximilian's unhappiness with Kalman Teitelman began the moment he showed up at the new rabbi's doorstep for his first bar mitzvah lesson. "Don't worry, Maxie," his mother had assured him, "everybody dislikes or distrusts what they're not familiar with; you'll get over it very soon, I'm sure." But it was more than dislike or distrust in Max's case. It was the feeling in the pit of his stomach when this strangest of strangers opened his apartment door, less a fear of what lay ahead than a deep longing for what was gone, gone forever. Even as the Lubavitcher held out a hand in greeting and said "Hello," the friendly image of Rabbi Kaminsky flashed before the boy's eyes, and he found himself wishing "If only ... if only...." A whole new beginning, thought Max; I don't know him, he doesn't know me. To the boy, the distance between the two personalities, his own and the rabbi's, was a boundless expanse of untraceable rivers and uncharted shorelines. One had only to *look* at the man to understand this!

There had been little time since he'd arrived for Rabbi Teitelman to be briefed on the seventy-five or eighty individuals who made up his congregation. Though Zelig Peikes had furnished him, that first day, with a hastily typed membership list together with a capsule commentary on the local "Who's Who," the children of the community were listed separately with nothing revealed beyond their names and dates of birth. Those simple statistics were all Rabbi Teitelman had learned thus far about his new pupil. As for what the pupil knew about his teacher, less could be said, for whatever initial impressions Max's family had gained they chose to exchange among themselves in Yiddish.

The boy's eyes now took in the rabbi's small apartment with a single quick sweep. It was located downtown, in the unfashionable district close to the synagogue, in keeping with Rabbi Teitelman's request, in one of a row of rundown frame houses whose front lawns, no larger than postage stamps, were littered with tricycles, baby carriages, and toys, all of which had seen better days. The inside of the apartment reminded Max of a cell, so sparse were its furnishings — an old oak desk, a bookcase, a couple of wooden folding chairs, a rocking chair that Max figured must have been sat in by Noah while waiting for the floodwaters to recede. A couple of gooseneck reading lamps provided the only lighting. There were no drapes, only thin curtains, but there was something rectangular on the floor — a rug — with splotches of pattern here and there, a stubborn reminder that it had once upon a time been a genuine Persian carpet.

"Not much here to inspire a young man, is there?" the rabbi said good-naturedly.

Maximilian remained silent, but it occurred to him that a day or two spent at A. Glick & Son's might prove to be a real eye-opener for the rabbi.

"Well," Rabbi Teitelman went on, trying to be jovial, "the scriptures bid us walk humbly with our God, but I go a step further, you see. I sit humbly with Him, and sleep even more humbly." Through the open door of the rabbi's bedroom, the boy spotted a narrow cot, made up army-style, with not so much as a wrinkle in the blanket. "Humbleness in the sight of God is one of the first lessons a man must learn, Maximilian."

Here it comes, thought Maximilian Glick, one of those boring lectures, like Mr. Sterling, the principal of his public school, was so fond of delivering at morning assemblies.

When the rabbi suddenly dropped the subject, Max was somewhat relieved. "Tell me something about yourself, Maximilian. All I know at the moment is that you're twelve-going-on-thirteen; and, God willing, before we know it you'll be at the magic age of manhood!"

Max nodded. Like a prisoner of war he decided to volunteer only the bare facts — name, rank, serial number.

"Any hobbies?" asked the rabbi. "I'm told you can't become a citizen of Steelton unless you play hockey in the winter, baseball in the summer, and football in the fall."

Maximilian resented the idea that he should be lumped together with a mass of sports-loving citizenry because of some country-style claptrap fed into the rabbi's brain. "I play the piano," he said. "I was in the Grade Eight piano course, but I skipped to Grade Ten after I won the top prize at the Steelton Music Festival."

It was only after this response had passed the boy's lips that he realized he'd boasted. He wished for a split second that he could recall his words, the way automobile factories recall defective cars. But then he thought: So what? So I boasted a little. Why not? It's something to be proud of. This funny-looking guy might as well know right now that he's not dealing with some ordinary puck-pusher.

Rabbi Teitelman smiled slyly.

"Did I say something funny?" Maximilian asked, increasingly unhappy over the turn the first interview was taking.

"No, nothing funny." The rabbi smiled again. "You said something very impressive, Maximilian. Very impressive indeed. Obviously you are a young man of special accomplishments — "

Darn right I am! Maximilian said to himself, feeling a little more secure now that he had established the fact.

"However ... " — the rabbi paused, still smiling, but now with a tinge of sadness — "don't you think it would have been even *more* impressive if you had left it to *me* to find out about your great success on my own?"

Suddenly the room struck Maximilian Glick as very hot and stuffy. He could feel his face burning, his shirtcollar damp at the back of his neck.

Was this a deliberate attempt by the new rabbi to cut him

down to size? Was all that earlier stuff about humility intended for him? Maximilian was convinced the answer to both questions was decidedly yes. Well, he thought, so this is how it begins, with a declaration of war.

The rest of the first hour was a strain. The rabbi, perhaps realizing he had overplayed his hand, tried bravely to lighten the tone of the lesson. But Max sat stolidly on one of the wooden folding chairs, across the desk from his teacher, betraying not the slightest emotion as Teitelman strove to make the coming bar mitzvah program sound stimulating and challenging.

"Your bar mitzvah falls ... let me see now — " the rabbi consulted a list of his pupils' birthdays, then his enthusiasm gave way to a look of disappointment, "September...."

"Something wrong with September?" asked Maximilian.

"Not really. It's just that I was hoping it fell in May."

"Why May?"

"I'm being selfish, I guess. My own was in May. It would have been fun — at least for *me* — to relive my experience through you. My Torah portion was taken from the Book of Numbers. That's not the telephone book of numbers, but one of the five books of Moses." Rabbi Teitelman chuckled at his own quip, but then, realizing that he was laughing alone, he said: "I gather you've heard that joke before."

"Many times," said Max matter-of-factly. Grandfather Glick used that line every chance he got at the Glick family dinner-table. Maximilian didn't mind laughing at a worn-out joke when his grandfather told it, but he was in no mood to extend the same courtesy to this man.

Shoring up his courage with a tuneless whistle, the young rabbi gazed up at the ceiling and squeezed his eyes shut, as if reading from an imaginary chart. "If my memory serves me correctly," he said slowly, "my Torah portion described the various numbers of Israelite males who were recorded when God ordered Moses to take a census in the second year following the Jews' exodus from Egypt. To be recorded you had to be twenty years of age and up, and able to bear arms.

From the tribe of Reuben there were 46,500. From the tribe of Simeon, 59,300. There were 45,650 from the tribe of Gad, 74,600 from Judah's tribe, 54,400 from Issachar's tribe ... uh ... from the tribe of Zebulun ... uh, 57,400 ... or was it 57,500? — "

Scratching his head, the rabbi went to his bookcase, withdrew the well-worn volume of the five books of Moses, and leafed his way swiftly to the precise passage. He grinned and looked over at the boy. "Ah, I was right the first time. The correct figure for the tribe of Zebulun is indeed 57,400. An elephant never forgets!"

Without quite realizing what he was saying, Maximilian challenged him. "I thought elephants were also expected to walk humbly with their God."

Caught with his own pride showing, Rabbi Teitelman all of a sudden looked grave. "Your point is well taken Mr. Glick. Tonight I will have to say a special prayer for *both* of us."

That's two strikes against you, Teitelman, Max said to himself. One more and you're out! The way Maximilian Glick saw it at the moment, he himself wasn't in need of any special prayers.

Seeking once again, this time a bit desperately, to pin a set of wings on their earthbound relationship, the young rabbi now forced a bright smile and tone of voice. "And now, Mr. Maximilian Glick, so much for lesson number one. Where are you off to now?"

"My dad's store."

"Excellent. Then we're headed in the same direction. I have an errand to do at the synagogue. We'll walk together."

Before Max had time to concoct a suitable excuse to avoid the rabbi's company, Teitelman had removed his skullcap and donned his wide-brimmed black hat and black frock coat. A minute later, the boy found himself on a street he'd known practically all his young life, walking side by side with this strange apparition of a man, this eye-catching, attention-getting ensemble of clothing and beard and sidelocks, this ghost from a time long past, from a place as remote as the dark side of the moon. Though the side-street was fairly deserted at this late afternoon hour, it seemed to the boy that a thousand eyes were on him, that hundreds of tongues wagged behind his back, that behind the windows of all the houses people stole glances, pointed, and snickered.

The two walked briskly, but to Max it seemed the longest walk he had ever taken. Miles!

And then they rounded the corner and found themselves on King Street, just a block from A. Glick & Son's. Unable to face being part of a two-man parade down the town's principal thoroughfare, Max thought quickly. "I just remembered something, Rabbi. My mother told me to pick up a loaf of bread at the bakery before I go home. That's it across the street. So, if you'll excuse me — "

"Of course, Maximilian. Goodnight. It was nice meeting you. I guess we'll be seeing a great deal of each other in the future."

"I guess so," said Max, without the slightest enthusiasm. "Goodnight." He sprinted across the street toward the bakery. But as he drew closer, Maximilian Glick realized that he had blundered, for in the shop, staring at him through the windows as if he too were now from some other planet, was a cluster of his schoolmates. He turned, as if to pass by, but it was no use. He was committed. The rabbi stood across the street, waving goodbye. Max had no choice now. He took a deep breath and entered.

When one expects the worst, one is seldom disappointed.

"Hey, Glick," said one of Maximilian's schoolmates, "where'd ya dig up the Black Phantom?"

"Isn't that guy kinda early for Hallowe'en?" another called.

"Frankenstein and Glickenstein," a third cried out. "Help! Save me! Save me!"

Maximilian Glick looked desperately about him. Laughter was coming from everywhere. Loaves of bread on the shelves, jelly rolls, pies, and cakes, everything seemed to be convulsed, cackling and snickering with malicious glee. The donuts, dozens of them arranged on large pans, had twisted themselves into row upon row of grinning mouths. Worst of all, one of the youths in the bakery was none other than Bobby Rosenberg who could afford to laugh the hardest because, as he now took pains to point out, he was two years older and had been lucky enough to be tutored for his bar mitzvah by Rabbi Kaminsky.

"You know something, Glick," said Bobby Rosenberg, loud enough for everyone, from the cashier at the front of the bakery to the pastry chef at the rear, to hear, "for a kid whose last name means 'good luck' you sure blew it today."

Later that evening, Maximilian, before going to bed, asked Henry Glick: "Dad, if 'Glick' is the Jewish word for good luck, what's the Jewish word for bad luck?"

"Umglick," Henry Glick answered. "Why?"

"No special reason. I was just wondering — "

In the middle of the night Maximilian had a dream. He was a soldier, a prisoner of war under interrogation. A faceless enemy officer was barking at him: "Name, rank, serial number ... name, rank, serial number!"

"Umglick," Maximilian, the hopeless hapless captive, could only answer. "Maximilian Umglick."

9

Throughout the deepening days of autumn, Maximilian had made his way to the Lubavitcher's apartment every Monday and Thursday after school for private bar mitzvah lessons. Somehow, on Mondays and Thursdays, the skies over Steelton hung heavier and grayer, the trees looked barer, their fallen leaves deader. And somehow, when winter came, landing heavily on both feet, the season seemed to save its iciest blasts for Mondays and Thursdays. On those days, even when Max tried not to inhale, needles of cold shot up through his nostrils and bored holes in his skull just behind his eyes. By the time he reached the rabbi's doorstep he was looking at the world through a silvery film of frost.

To make matters worse, the rabbi's apartment was as uninviting on a late wintry afternoon as the inside of a boxcar. Nowhere within that hard little rectangle of living space was there a single stick of furniture that offered warmth and comfort. The wooden folding chairs, the oak desk, the gooseneck lamp — all conveyed one message: "Let's get on with it."

And that was precisely the spirit in which Maximilian carried on, Mondays and Thursdays, week after week. Each and every lesson, scheduled to last sixty minutes, began promptly on the hour, and ended not a minute late. Max showed up on time, homework done, lessons learned. He chanted the traditional Hebrew prayers in a boyish tenor that was clear and steady, unlike most youngsters his age whose voices caromed from one corner of the musical scale to another like pinballs. Ask Maximilian to recite the thirty-nine acts an Orthodox Jew was forbidden to perform on the Sabbath, and in thirty-nine seconds flat you were told "Ploughing, sowing, reaping, sheaf-making," and thirty-five more.

So mechanical was all this, so devoid of spontaneity or surprise, that Maximilian composed a poem in his head, and trudged to and fro on Mondays and Thursdays to its rhythm:

Press a button, hear a click,
It's time for Maximilian Glick.

Time for numbers, time for dates,
Time for measures, time for weights.

Remember the cities, remember the states,
And the prophets who rose up through Heaven's gates.

Keep it simple and clipped like grass,
With patience and luck this too will pass.

So Max be nimble, Max be quick,
Remember you're Maximilian Glick!

Punctuality and proficiency ... they were apparently the only virtues the Lubavitcher looked for, and they were all he would get, as far as Maximilian Glick was concerned. Punctuality, proficiency.

But these were qualities that great bank clerks or night watchmen were made of. Great scholars? — No. And nobody understood this better than the young Lubavitcher rabbi. How many times, in his years of training, had Kalman Teitelman's teachers drummed it into him that learning began with a spark; then came imagination, fanning the spark like a bellows; finally the fire itself, glowing when teacher and pupil began to forge a friendship. How many times had Kalman Teitelman been cautioned by *his* teachers that the most me-

ticulous scholarship, the most faithful fulfilment of God's commandments, were empty if there was no passion. But in the
case of Maximilian Glick, the rabbi's oldest pupil and his one
and only bar mitzvah candidate, all these things were absent.
No spark, no bellows, no fire. "We are like two robots," he
lamented to himself. "Hello, goodbye, nothing more."

Studying himself in the bathroom mirror — a private act
of vanity the young rabbi occasionally indulged in — he mur-
mured: "Look at you .... a man at home in two alphabets;
you can add, subtract, multiply, and divide; you're blessed
with the power of reason and a leakproof memory; you've
inherited a faith that's as ancient as the hills. And yet, to this
twelve-year-old, this kid who looks at you with sidelong glances,
what are you? No more than a mound of mashed potatoes,
making pious noises and gestures that rise up and disappear
like so much steam."

Leaning more closely into the mirror, the Lubavitcher pulled
his skin down tight over his cheekbones so that his face became a grotesque mask. "Yes ... yes, Teitelman, your flesh is
too pale, your blood too invisible." Turning from the mirror
image, the Lubavitcher brought his soliloquy to a final passionate resolve. "I must put *life* into this relationship! But
how?"

Several days passed, and still Rabbi Teitelman could find
no solution to his problem. He had prayed. He had searched
his soul for an answer to the question "How?" He had prayed
again and longer, and when the answer was not forthcoming,
he had prayed more fervently, remembering always an old
Lubavitcher saying: "You are praying correctly when you are
so absorbed that you do not feel a knife thrust into your
body."

Then, in the mail one morning, there arrived a crisp white
envelope addressed to "Reverend K. Teitelman." In its upper
left-hand corner, two lions, each on its hind legs, faced one
another angrily, engaged in a fight to the death; beneath ran
a banner across which was printed in Old English lettering,
"Labor Omnia Vincit." Above the lions, embossed in gold,

were the words "Office of The Mayor, City of Steelton." The rabbi, presuming its contents to be something more than an invitation to pay taxes, opened the envelope carefully.

Inside was a crisp white note, neatly typed, signed in a careless blue scrawl befitting the sender's high office —

Reverend Sir:

As you are no doubt aware, the City of Steelton is proud to number among its native sons the noted author and humorist, and recent recipient of the prestigious Governor General's Award for Literary Humor, Buckner Finsterwald.

In recognition of Mr. Finsterwald's acclaimed achievements in his field, and upon the occasion of his sixtieth birthday, the City of Steelton, of which I have the privilege of being Mayor, will tender a reception in Mr. Finsterwald's honor on Wednesday night, January 14th next, in the Auditorium of Steelton Collegiate Institute.

Tributes will be paid to our honored guest by a number of prominent dignitaries, including the Minister of Culture for this Province.

It will be my special pleasure to present Mr. Finsterwald with the key to the City and to announce the creation of the Buckner Finsterwald Annual Scholarship Fund, established by an act of the City Council, which fund will provide a yearly prize of fifty dollars to a student of Steelton Collegiate Institute who submits the best humorous essay.

Following ceremonies in the Auditorium, there will be refreshments, and Mr. Finsterwald has kindly consented to autograph copies of his new book, *Pleasure Before Business*, a collection of rollicking tales recommended for busy executives and people in public life.

We have invited your colleagues of the cloth, The Very Reverend Kingston Salisbury Archer, Bishop of the Anglican Diocese of Steelton, and Reverend Monsignor Jean-Paul O'Neil, Rector of the Sanctuary of the Precious Blood, to grace our stage, and to participate in the opening invocation. We would be especially pleased, particularly since Mr. Finsterwald is

also of the Hebrew persuasion, if you would join in the opening portion of the ceremonies, making a contribution which I
am certain will be unique because of the common Faith which
our honored guest shares with you.

To assist our Committee in making final arrangements,
your earliest possible response is respectfully requested.
Faithfully,
J. Lawson Perkins,
Mayor.

That afternoon, Maximilian Glick took his seat precisely
as the hands of his watch touched four, and opened his notebook to the latest page of homework.

"One moment, Maximilian, before we begin — " Rabbi
Teitelman said. "I need a favor from you, something you can
do for me, if you will." He handed his pupil the letter from
Mayor Perkins, waited while he read the invitation half-aloud,
then explained: "I've accepted the invitation, and even though
I've never before participated in this kind of thing ... I mean,
being on a stage with a bishop and a priest ... I think it's
clearly my duty to represent the Jewish congregation ... especially since Buckner Finsterwald is apparently one of *us*."

"Yes," Maximilian responded with only mild interest.

"There's just one problem, Maximilian," the rabbi went
on. "I've never *heard* of Mr. Buckner Finsterwald. Am I right
to assume that *you* have?"

"Everybody in Steelton has heard of Buckner Finsterwald.
We've got most of his books at home. One of his books is in
our English course at school this year, the one about when
he was growing up. It's called *Forged In Steelton: The Crucible of Boyhood*. Our English teacher says it's a masterpiece.
My mom and dad think he's terrific too."

"And do you agree?"

"Honest?"

"Honest — "

"I think Buckner Finsterwald stinks."

Rabbi Teitelman's eyebrows rose. "Really, Maximilian?
Why?"

"Because he says a whole lot of really dumb things as far as I'm concerned."

"Like what?"

"Like how his mom was always so great and wise; and even though they were so poor they could only afford meat once a week, they were all happy as pigs because it was fun living in one room behind their dry-cleaning shop . . . a lot of stuff like that."

"And you don't believe Mr. Finsterwald?" the rabbi asked.

"Nobody in his right mind would enjoy being poor and hungry all the time, and living in a sardine can, which is the way he described their home. And I don't believe his mom never blew her cool when his father brought a family of Italian immigrants home for supper one Friday night, without warning her in advance, and the whole gang — the Finsterwalds and the Italians — shared one tiny little chicken."

Rabbi Teitelman fought back an impulse to laugh. "I see a side to you, Mr. Glick, that I never knew existed. You, my friend, are a cynic."

"What's a cynic?"

"A cynic is a person who refuses to look at the world through rose-colored glasses."

Maximilian smiled. He hadn't known before that he was a cynic, and the description did not displease him. "Well," he offered, "wouldn't *you* be a cynic if you read what Finsterwald wrote about how to keep Jewishness alive in our times?"

"Try me. What did Mr. Finsterwald write?"

"He says that if he had his way he'd manufacture aerosol cans filled with chicken soup. Then Jews could spray Jewishness around their houses, the way they do with air fresheners. I mean, is that weird, or is that *weird*!"

The rabbi managed a straight face. "Not only is it weird; think what it would do to the earth's ozone layer! Anyway, Maximilian, ours is not to reason why, ours is but to do and die. So I want you to do me a favor. The ceremony takes place in less than two weeks and that doesn't give me much time to bone up on Buckner Finsterwald. I wonder if you could do some of the research for me ... maybe get me one or two of his books from the library so I can skim through them ... get some kind of feel for the man and his background. Do you think you could manage that?"

"I can tell you one thing now about his background that I heard," Maximilian said with a sly smile.

"Good. Tell me."

"Well, every time he comes to town — which isn't often now that he's such a big shot — he goes through this phony thing of telling everybody to call him 'Bucky,' not 'Buckner,' which is supposed to make everybody think he's a real friendly down-to-earth guy, right? But when he was here a couple of years ago, he made a speech at the synagogue and afterward a lot of people asked him to sign his autograph, and he refused except if they handed him one of his books to sign. I mean, he wouldn't even sign copies of the *program*. My grandmother and my mom had one of their famous fights over it. My grandmother said old Finsterwald was a prize snob, and then my mother said she didn't blame him because that's how writers make their living, selling books, not giving free autographs. My mother said the trouble with people was that they always want something for nothing. Then my grandmother got *really* sore and said she always paid her own way in this world. And then they had an awful fight, so awful they started saying things to each other in *Jewish*."

"Very interesting," the rabbi said thoughtfully, "Very interesting indeed. However, maybe we'd better stick to straight historical facts, eh Maximilian? Maybe you can find out the exact spot in Steelton where he was born ... where he was educated, where and how he got his start. ... Of course," the Lubavitcher added in a cautious sing-song, "if you happen ... just accidentally, say ... to run across any more of those anecdotes in the course of your research — what shall we call them, human interest angles?" — Max immediately brightened — "You might throw in one or two of them, just to make the sauce a little spicier, eh?"

So eager did the boy now appear to get on with this assignment that the Lubavitcher felt bound to add quickly: "Mind you, Max, my remarks have to be appropriate to an invocation, you understand. I can't for instance say 'Dear God, bless all of us who are assembled here to do honor to this big shot who calls himself Bucky but is really a prize snob.'"

For the first time since they'd met, Maximilian found himself laughing at something the Lubavitcher said. For the first time too, Max's afternoon lesson ran past the sacred sixty-minute mark by a full quarter-hour, a fact that didn't seem to upset either teacher or pupil at all.

Standing by his livingroom window, hands clasped behind his back, the Lubavitcher rabbi watched his pupil slog through freshly fallen snow, his toqued head almost obliterated by clouds of breath. Suddenly, at the first lamppost, Maximilian turned and glanced up.

The Lubavitcher and the boy gave no sign that they saw each other, but in that blink or two of the eye, in that moment before the boy turned away, Rabbi Teitelman thought he could hear a faint whisper, the answer to his question.

10

In the faces of the dignitaries who marched on stage at Steelton High on the night of January fourteenth, one thing was clear: their presence here tonight was a mistake.

The tribute to Buckner Finsterwald ought to have consisted of a visit to the Mayor's Office, a brief ceremony before City Council, a photograph or two, thank you very much and goodbye. Instead, Mayor Perkins, inspired by some vague notion that Finsterwald's success was due largely to his having been born and raised in a melting-pot society, had sponsored a special resolution — which Council dutifully made unanimous — that the tribute be expanded into "Steelton Brotherhood Day." Taking stock of the platitudes stored in the cellars of his rhetoric, the Mayor selected several vintages that went down well with consecrations and dedications. In a proclamation blended with portions of the Magna Carta and the Gettysburg Address, laced with part of a eulogy he himself had delivered years before at his predecessor's funeral, Mayor Perkins exhorted the citizenry to reaffirm those principles that had made them strong and united — Equality, Fraternity, and Mankind's Infinite Capacity for Love.

The trouble with this exhortation was simply that it defied the basic rule of survival in Steelton. In the minds of the ordinary citizens, the social climate of the city fell into the same category as the seasonal climate — an ongoing act of God best endured with a maximum of resignation, a minimum of talk. The proposition that all men were created equal made about as much sense as a proposal to plant banana trees on the courthouse lawn. Indeed, any trumpet call to unity succeeded only in awakening people to the differences and disparities that kept them apart. It was as if an itinerant freak show had been invited to town to remind them of mankind's infinite capacity to be privileged and unprivileged. Even among the Mayor's earnest councillors, the intoxication caused by his opening pronouncements soon changed to a deadly sobriety.

Still, a commitment was a commitment. Nothing to do now but see this thing through. That was the spirit very much evident among the party recruited to join Buckner Finsterwald on stage. Grim as a firing squad, they stood at attention as Miss Klemenhoog made her way — largely on foot, as was her keyboard style — through two choruses of "Land of Hope and Glory" (a touch of Edwardian England that left little doubt as to who ran things in Steelton, brotherhood or no brotherhood). Amidst all the patent reserve, only the smile of Buckner Finsterwald — radiating practised charm and first-rate dentistry — gave evidence that a civic celebration was under way.

To the great man himself went the only armchair on stage, placed dead-center. To his and the Mayor's immediate right sat the colleagues of the cloth, Bishop Archer, Monsignor O'Neil, and Rabbi Teitelman, a trio of magpies on folding metal chairs waiting in silence for a signal to flap their wings, exchanging nothing brotherly between them but muffled coughs and periodic throat-clearings. Indeed, Finsterwald's backstage entreaties to them to call him "Bucky" had done nothing to lubricate their relationship with each other, and Finsterwald himself, accustomed in the past to the familiar face of Rabbi Kaminsky, seemed unable to come to terms with the young rabbi now seated near him. Rabbi Teitelman had discerned, by the way Finsterwald had earlier offered his hand, that the writer wondered whether or not he'd ever get it back.

To the left of Perkins and Finsterwald, pressing more pounds per square inch into her folding chair than it was designed to support, sat Gabriella Gabor-Mindesz, Honorary

Chairman of Steelton's Arts & Letters Society and recent widow of Tomas Gabor-Mindesz, the lumber baron. Childless and sole heir to her husband's fortune, Mrs. Gabor-Mindesz rattled about in a three-storey stone mansion on Pine Hill referred to as "City Hall" by neighbors who resented its overpowering presence. In the mahogany-paneled drawing-room of "City Hall" the mistress of the house presided over meetings of the Arts & Letters Society, as well as intimate chamber recitals and poetry readings. Despite her own massive dimensions (some locals referred to *her* as "City Hall") she had been the star, before World War Two, of a light opera company in Budapest. Though well into her sixties now, she comported herself as if all the world were still at her feet. Recognizing friends and beneficiaries in the audience, she dipped her bleached coiffure regally in their direction or waved a hand bedecked with enough diamonds to blind the sun. In memory of her husband, whose skull was fatally disarranged by an irreverent sheet of plywood at one of his lumber yards, Mrs. Gabor-Mindesz had made a substantial donation toward the costs of the Buckner Finsterwald Tribute, matching the city's contribution dollar for dollar.

To the left of Mrs. Gabor-Mindesz sat the province's Minister of Culture, the Honorable Claxton Thye, a middle-aged politician whose current portfolio was acknowledged in government circles to be the last hundred steps to oblivion. Thye stared out into the audience. His lips moved slightly, as if from long years of habit he was conducting a head-count to assess who was for him and who against. One he knew for certain to be hostile was Mayor Perkins, an opponent ever since the day Thye — then Minister of Public Works — refused to grant one cent of provincial tax money in aid of the Mayor's King–Queen Sewer Renewal Program. Apart from a perfunctory handshake backstage, the two men ignored each other.

Side by side, next to Claxton Thye, sat Drummond Quain, chairman of the steel plant's board of directors, and Scotty DiAngelo, president of the steelworkers' local (and skip of the champion Marconi Hall Curling Team). Only a few days earlier, after weeks of facing each other across a bargaining table, Quain had called DiAngelo a thug. DiAngelo had called Quain a pig. Now, a threatened strike less than forty-eight hours from becoming a reality, thug and pig squinted uneasily under the stagelights of the highschool auditorium, each pretending to be more at home than the other in a place from which neither had managed to graduate.

Besides occupying the only armchair on stage, Buckner Finsterwald was distinguished from those seated about him by his attire. If there is such a phenomenon as a writer's uniform, Finsterwald had refined it down to the last stitch. His jacket, shaped like a riding jacket to fit closely at the waist and flare at the side-vents, was cut of chocolatey velvet, one lapel set off by a discreet yellow *boutonnière.* His trousers were tailored in a harmonious glen check cloth. He wore a saffron silk shirt, open at the neck, its collar turned down over the collar of his jacket. Concealing his throat was a paisley ascot tied a bit on the loose side so that it appeared to flow down into his shirt like a waterfall. Finsterwald's hair, streaked with gray, white, and silver, stood out from his head in oceanic waves that monopolized the overhead lights, as if there was nothing else on stage worth illuminating. Obviously pleased at all the attention, Buckner Finsterwald made a point of turning his profile to the audience from time to time, exhibiting a long fine nose John Barrymore might have envied. Unlike the others, who sat stiffly and self-consciously, he lounged now in his modest throne, his legs crossed to reveal slender, rather feminine ankles, hands draped elegantly over one knee, ready to be kissed at a moment's notice.

With an air of command that had kept him in office for five successive terms, Mayor Perkins rose precisely at eight-thirty, advanced to the microphone on the lectern, and coughed the cough of a chief magistrate. His stance — hands pressed behind him into the small of his broad back, balding head lowered like a bulldog's — was remarkably Churchillian. His oratory, on the other hand, had but one virtue — predictability.

His Worship considered it a great privilege and pleasure ... as expected; he was both delighted and proud, and yet at the same time humble ... as expected; he was profoundly grateful, on behalf of the citizens of Steelton, for Mrs. Gabor-Mindesz's generous contribution not only to this event but to the cultural life of the city in general ... again, as expected. "What we have here," said His Worship, "is yet another example of men and women from all walks of life, pulling together to build a bigger and better community." Even Buckner Finsterwald unfolded his elegant hands long enough to join in the few seconds of self-congratulatory applause that filled the auditorium.

Then, on call, Bishop Archer took his place at the lectern. Eyes shut tightly, lips pursed in deep devotion, the portly Bishop besought "the Creator of us all ... and I do most sincerely mean all" to bestow His eternal goodness upon those assembled. At the words "and I do most sincerely mean all" Bishop Archer opened his eyes and nodded ostentatiously in the direction of Buckner Finsterwald. Finsterwald returned the courtesy, bowing his head as if he'd just received a hundred-dollar tip.

Now it was Monsignor Jean-Paul O'Neil's turn to invoke. In an odd accent, part Irish, part French Canadian, the tall leathery priest addressed the Holy Trinity in an easy intimate manner, as if They and he had been college chums. Pausing after each couple of sentences to run a hand through his white close-cropped hair, he seemed to be reminding Them that he was no youngster in this business either. "Father, Son, and Holy Spirit," he prayed, "grant Your blessings upon this gathering of good souls. . . ." Then, almost as an afterthought: "Without regard to race, color, or creed, of course."

Once again Mayor Perkins stood at the lectern. "And now, ladies and gentlemen ... to join in the invocation I call upon Rabbi Kalman Teitelman, spiritual leader of our good friends of Steelton's Hebrew community, with which splendid group of public-spirited citizens our distinguished guest Buckner Finsterwald —"

Oozing good nature, Finsterwald called out "Bucky ... Bucky —"

Accepting correction with similar good nature, Mayor Perkins continued: "*Bucky* ... with which splendid group of public-spirited citizens our distinguished guest *Bucky* Finsterwald remains bound in heart though his travels take him far and wide."

Up to the microphone stepped Rabbi Teitelman. From an inside pocket of his long black coat he took a sheet of foolscap, unfolded it, and laid it carefully on the lectern.

In the audience, Morris Moskover leaned across to Zelig Peikes. "What's wrong, Peikes; can't your man pray without notes?"

Weary from months of bearing the blame for the Lubavitcher, Peikes whispered angrily: "What do you think would've happened if Moses forgot to write down the Ten Commandments?"

"Life would have been a lot easier for everybody," said the Local Sage.

Harry Zwicker, the congregation's secretary, whispered to Peikes: "If only Kaminsky was alive tonight!"

Peikes said nothing, but in his heart he yearned for the impossible. If only he could have pressed a button, thereby transforming this misfit at the lectern into a fascimile of the late Rabbi Kaminsky. Surrounding Peikes and his fellow congregants — who sat in a pocket a few rows from the stage — was a steady hum subsiding only when the young Lubavitcher uttered his first sounds — a loud cough, a long noisy clearing of the throat.

"Mr. Mayor, Honored Guest, M'Lord Bishop, Reverend Monsignor, Distinguished Dignitaries...."

"What's he doing now," Moskover demanded of Peikes, "taking the census?"

"You're supposed to address these people by their proper titles," Peikes explained.

"Then how come the others didn't do it?"

"Ask *them*."

"How can I ask them?"

"Become an Anglican or a Catholic," said Peikes. "I'll see if I can arrange it first thing tomorrow morning."

Satisfied that at last he had everyone's attention, Rabbi Teitelman began in a quiet voice: "I have a confession to make. With Bishop Archer, Monsignor O'Neil, and finally me, standing on this stage asking the Almighty to grace these proceedings ... what you've received here tonight is at best a mixed blessing —"

From every quarter of the auditorium came laughter, every quarter, that is, except two: the stage and the embattled zone where the rabbi's congregants sat stunned by this unexpected levity.

"Speaking of confession," Teitelman continued, "I suppose what all of us here have most in common is that good old-fashioned sense of guilt that makes our world go round. The difference is that when a Protestant feels guilty about his sins, he climbs on a soap-box at a streetcorner and shouts his confession; a Catholic climbs *in*to a box and whispers his; a Jew, on the other hand, locks himself in the basement and writes his autobiography."

"Oh my God!" Moskover whispered in horror. "They'll never forgive us if we live a hundred years!"

Picking up steam, Teitelman rolled on: "That's one of the reasons we Jews are called 'People Of The Book.' But not the main reason. The main reason is that down through the ages somebody or other in authority has always thrown the book at us —"

Once again, the audience broke into appreciative applause. "Thank you, thank you very much." The rabbi bowed his head jerkily. Zelig Peikes buried his face in his hands. Several seats from Peikes, the wife of Milt Katzenberg grumbled: "What's he think this is, a nightclub?" Clearly, the rabbi's flock was not prepared for a shepherd who cracked jokes when confronted with an amplification system and a captive audience. Nor were the bishop and priest. Both squirmed in their skimpy chairs; both looked ecumenically baleful.

Confident now that he had the audience with him, totally blind to the agony among his own congregants, the young Lubavitcher ran on: "I'm from Boston ... where the famous Boston Tea Party took place. The American settlers objected to the British tax and dumped all their tea into Boston Harbor. Then the Jewish settlers threw in a little sugar and lemon and drank the whole thing. ..."

Teitelman paused to allow laughter to roll over him like a warm towel. "When I told my friends in Boston I was coming all the way up here to Steelton, they said I'd be bored to death in a town like this. They said Steelton was so boring that the *Steelton Star*, instead of publishing obituaries, publishes a list of who survived —"

Out there, beyond the footlights, the rabbi's own people were curdling with embarrassment, but the rabbi was still unaware — of them, of the Mayor and guest of honor sitting forward in their seats, their faces reflecting mounting anxiety over the direction this invocation was taking.

"I noted ... on this envelope" — Rabbi Teitelman took from his pocket the envelope from the Mayor's Office and held it aloft — "I noted that Steelton's emblem consists of two lions wrestling with each other. Nobody can tell which lion is Mr. Quain and which is Mr. DiAngelo, but it doesn't matter. The motto under the emblem reads 'Labor Omnia Vincit' ... 'Labor Conquers All' ... I guess that tells us whose side City Hall is on, doesn't it?"

This brought a wild cheer from a large segment of the audience, some jeering from a smaller segment, and inspired Scotty DiAngelo to rise from his chair and lift his arms in the gesture of a triumphant prizefighter. Drummond Quain glared at the Lubavitcher, then turned and scowled at Mayor Perkins who pretended not to notice.

"How appropriate it is," said Teitelman, "that we have with us this evening the Provincial Minister of Culture ... a man who has done so much to keep the culture of Steelton provincial —"

Claxton Thye now joined the expanding brotherhood of

unhappiness. As Minister of Culture he'd been as ungenerous to the Finsterwald tribute as he'd been to Mayor Perkins's sewage dreams when Minister of Public Works. As far as he was concerned, his presence alone was a sufficient contribution to the event. But this circumstance had not yet been revealed to the local press for reasons of taste, and Thye wondered how on earth it could have been leaked to — of all people — this outlandish rabbi.

Again Zelig Peikes found himself being buried under a hailstorm of advice.

Morris Moskover leaned toward him. "Peikes, do something, *say* something. He's ruining us!"

"Make a signal," Milt Katzenberg whispered. "Wave your handkerchief."

"Handkerchief nothing!" said Harry Zwicker. "Stand up and tell him to sit down."

"I can't do that," Peikes protested.

"Why not?" said Katzenberg. "Who pays his salary?"

"Don't send him this month's cheque!" Moskover said to Katzenberg.

"Look who's giving orders," Katzenberg shot back. "You still owe last year's dues, Moskover."

Caught in this crossfire, Peikes was almost relieved when Rabbi Teitelman's voice broke in.

"A word now about our benefactor . . ." Teitelman directed his attention to Mrs. Gabor-Mindesz. "Or should I say bene-*factory*, bearing in mind that Steelton's culture will never slumber so long as there's Mindesz Lumber —"

Applause and laughter.

"Commercials he's doing now!" said Katzenberg.

Peikes and his band smouldered.

"That's all I need," moaned Sam Lipicoff, a competitor of the late Tomas Gabor-Mindesz, whose own company, Lipicoff Lumber, was on thin ice twelve months of the year.

On stage, the dignitaries were struggling to maintain their composure. Mrs. Gabor-Mindesz, unamused by the rabbi's rhyme, fanned herself vigorously with a copy of her speech.

Thrown together in adversity, Bishop Archer and Monsignor O'Neil conferred behind a raised program. Only Scotty DiAngelo, union leader, glowed with satisfaction, no doubt reading into the rabbi's new interpretation of his hometown motto signs of future victories at the picket lines.

For dramatic effect, the Lubavitcher halted his invocation long enough to pour himself a glass of water. After a quick gulp, he turned toward the guest of honor, Buckner Finsterwald. "About Buckner Finsterwald ... *Bucky* Finsterwald ... there is much to be said —"

"Please, *please* God, don't let him say it," Augustus Glick prayed.

"Amen!" Peikes added.

The Lubavitcher paused again to steal a glance at his notes. "This native son ... forged in Steelton, as he so dramatically puts it in his autobiography ... this man for whom the crucible of boyhood was a simmering vat of chicken soup ... except that as the Great Depression wore on, all his family could afford was a *photograph* of chicken soup clipped from a magazine —"

Sarah Glick frowned at Henry Glick. "That wasn't in the book, was it? I don't remember anything like that."

Henry Glick could not bring himself to speak.

"And yet ... and yet, ladies and gentlemen ... despite the constant presence of the wolf at their door ... not an ordinary wolf mind you, but Sol Wolfe, their landlord at the time —"

In the audience, Millie Wolfe, spinster-daughter of the late Sol Wolfe, whose shabby building had once housed the hollow-bellied Finsterwalds, groaned: "How the devil would Teitelman have known that!"

Teitelman carried on: "In the face of manifold tribulations and deprivations, the humor of Buckner Finsterwald ... *Bucky* ... bubbled up from the deepest and most traditional wellsprings of Jewish wit — Turmoil and Mineral Oil. ..."

"Shocking! Absolutely shocking!" Reva Skolnick, president of the Jewish Women's Auxiliary, hissed.

Under the glare of the overhead stagelights, Buckner Finsterwald, once so composed, so full of his own eminence, the sheen of his garb reflecting the sheen of his reputation, now commenced to age, to wilt and shrivel like Dorian Gray before the spectators' eyes. Was this his sixtieth birthday? His seventieth? His hundredth? His eyes, fixed upon the young rabbi at the lectern, pleaded that the invocation end.

A few rows from the stage, Zelig Peikes too fixed his gaze upon the rabbi with the same desperation, hoping to catch the rabbi's eye, to convey with a subtle motion of the head or a barely perceptible frown the urgency of stopping before all was lost — all those years of leaving well enough alone, all the itchy areas of Steelton life, all the rashes, the benign tumors, now suddenly exposed by this unpredictable monologist. And as for Peikes himself, the past few minutes had seen his lengthy presidential career plummet from twilight into a netherworld. "After tonight," he said to himself, "I'll be lucky to be elected dog-catcher."

Teitelman, however, had seen and heard only the applause and laughter of a demonstrative majority. "May I close my few remarks —"

"Thank God!" said Zelig Peikes.

"May I close my few remarks by calling now upon the God of Abraham, Isaac, and Jacob, all praise be to Him, to make His countenance to shine upon us and give us peace . . . all of us . . . regardless of race, color, or creed, of course. Amen."

Folding his notes, Teitelman restored them to the inside pocket of his coat. In shoes the size of barges, he shuffled across the stage to his seat, pausing only long enough to acknowledge a final round of applause with the characteristic jerky bow of his head. On either side of him, the dignitaries sat like granite statues, as though frozen for all time. Only Scotty DiAngelo displayed flesh and blood, chuckling to himself, reveling in the opening of someone else's wounds, the ruffling of someone else's feathers, the pricking of someone else's balloons.

At the rear of the auditorium, behind the last-row seats in the dark standing-room section, was one citizen of Steelton for whom the moment was filled only with unspeakable pleasure — Maximilian Glick.

The boy had slipped into the auditorium after the audience was seated and the house lights dimmed. Slipping away now as unobtrusively, he started for home, taking deep breaths, letting the bracing night air expand the feeling of pride in his chest. After all, had he not provided grist for the rabbi's mill? And the applause — Maximilian understood applause. Applause was food and drink. Applause was approval, gratitude, *love*. Applause was something offered to one in a hundred, one in a thousand! How many people ever knew the sound of it, the sight of it, the very taste of it!

11

The day after Steelton Brotherhood Day — a Thursday —
began for Rabbi Teitelman like most others. At dawn his cheap
old-fashioned alarm clock kept up the irritating noise that
always made him feel as though he were being regimented to
daily toil in a salt mine.

After morning prayers there was a simple breakfast: a
piece of fruit, a three-minute egg, tea (black, no sugar). Saturday morning's sermon was only half-written; to complete
it took another couple of hours of study and writing. Then
there was Sunday morning's weekly bible story to prepare
for the kindergarten class, always a chore because it neces-
sitated squeezing the cruelty of oppressors, the evil of sin-
ners, and the wrath of God through a fine strainer until they
were reduced to innocent babyfood.

Lunch was a scoop of cottage cheese, fruit again, tea again.

At Steelton General Hospital there was a visit to Mrs.
Shainhouse whose gallstones rested in a sealed jar on her
night-table, preserved as testimony to the patient's bravery
and her surgeon's vanity. Then on to Nathan Pripchik, recu-
perating from a hernia operation, and an interminable history of poor Pripchik's symptoms, surgery, and hair-raising
after-effects. Leaving the wards at last, he made up his mind
that hospital visitations were really the business of Christian
missionaries, not rabbis.

Having no appetite now for food or drink, the rabbi fore-
went his usual mid-afternoon snack (more fruit, more tea,

this time with lemon). Instead, he immersed himself in the Torah portion for the coming Sabbath, thankful that nowhere in the text for that week was there to be found a single reference to any part of the human anatomy.

Promptly at four o'clock the rabbi opened the door of his apartment to admit an ebullient Max.

"Hi. You were great!" Maximilian chirped.

"Great? What're you talking about?"

"Last night. I sneaked into the auditorium. Caught the whole show. I scored it ten for Teitelman, zero for Finsterwald. I hear he still sold a lot of books afterward, though."

"Tons."

"That's probably because everybody felt sorry for him," said Max.

Teitelman shook his head remorsefully. "I don't know what got into me. Somewhere inside me there's a fool."

"The audience loved it."

"Not all of them, unfortunately. I ran into Mr. Peikes in the lobby. You should've seen the look on his face. As for the people on the stage, you'd think I had leprosy. The only person who spoke to me was that union fellow, DiAngelo." Teitelman shook his head again. "I don't know *what* got into me."

Maximilian was determined to see the bright side. "Well as far as I'm concerned you were terrific. I don't care what people are saying."

"What are people saying, Max? Your folks, for instance . . . what are they saying?"

"I don't know, but whatever it is, they're saying it in Yiddish."

"I see," said the Lubavitcher. He paused to weigh this bad news.

"Can I ask you a question?" Max said.

Teitelman smiled. "So long as it's not personal."

"What *did* get into you?"

The rabbi reflected for a moment. "The same thing that got into me when I was about your age. One day, at cheder, a

Lubavitch kid like myself leaned across the aisle and whispered: 'Hey, Teitelman, know what God said when Moses had a headache? — Moses, take two tablets.' I laughed out loud, and we both got into big trouble. Ended up cleaning off every blackboard in school. But I was never quite the same after that. I thought to myself: it was worth it; one good laugh is worth twenty blackboards. I guess you could say that during the rest of my academic career I majored in blackboards. The day I graduated they rolled my doghouse into the assembly so they could hand me my diploma."

Teitelman laughed. For the first time, Maximilian noted that Teitelman's laugh — unlike Rabbi Kaminsky's, which had been deep and from the chest — seemed to come from somewhere behind his thin nose, traveling a much shorter route to the open air and emerging in rapid metallic bursts, like machinegun-fire.

"You know any more of those?" Maximilian asked.

"More of which?"

"Jokes like take-two-tablets — "

"I'll let you in on a little secret, Mr. Glick. But first you must promise not to breathe a word of this; otherwise God help you. Okay?"

Max started to cross his heart, then thought better of it. "Promise," he said.

"The truth is, I have a million of 'em. You see, by the time I had reached my teens, the one thing I really wanted to be was a comedy writer. You must understand something, Max: my father is a Lubavitcher rabbi; so was his father, in the old country, in Poland. My older brother who lives in Cleveland is a Lubavitcher rabbi. Also my two uncles in Los Angeles. You get the picture? Well, there was a whole world outside the Teitelman household, and I felt like a shut-in, pressing my nose against the windowpane, watching all the 'free' people out there running and playing and doing as they pleased. So, I had to smuggle joke books into my bedroom and hide them. And I spent hours making up new jokes. And I thought to myself: Some day, Kalman Teitelman, you're gonna be Neil

Simon and Woody Allen and Mel Brooks all rolled into one. I was even going to change my name. Kal Title. Or Kelly Title. Great huh?"

"What happened?"

Teitelman sighed. "I guess it was inevitable. One day my father discovered my joke books and the notebooks where I'd scribbled a bunch I'd made up. He did the worst thing imaginable, Max; he *didn't* have a temper tantrum. Instead, he handed them back to me ... very quietly; then he went into his study, put his head down on his arms, and wept ... very quietly. All the rest of that day and most of the next he fasted. It was like I had died and he was in mourning."

Maximilian looked puzzled. "I don't understand. You once told me that Lubavitchers believe in joy ... that they like to dance and sing, and even drink at celebrations. I remember what you said ... that they believe in putting lots of spirit into worship so that even the commonest man — and not just the richest or the most educated — can feel close to God."

"Ah yes, so I did. But ... and it's an important but ... we also believe in being very learned. Ignorance is *not* bliss, Maximilian. And we believe in strict obedience to many of the old rules about Jewish social and religious life. To put it plainly, Maximilian, we just don't play around."

"And your family thought you were just playing around?"

"Alas, yes." Rabbi Teitelman tilted his chair back a bit, at the same time shifting his small black skullcap forward on his head so it wouldn't fall off. "Anyway, bad news always travels fast. Before I could utter another one-liner, my older brother was on the phone from Cleveland followed by both uncles from Los Angeles ... long distance — person-to-person! — begging me to save what was left of my soul and saying things like 'How can you do this to your father?' and other comments designed to make me feel like I had invented the Golden Calf. I'll spare you all the horrible details after that series of phone calls, Mr. Glick. It's enough to say that they won, I lost, and here I am in Steelton, pouring out my confession to a twelve-year-old piano player. You want me to let you in on another secret, while I'm at it?"

"Yes!" By now Maximilian was eager to hear more from the man he'd once looked on as a clam in a black suit.

"Not a word about this, remember?"

"Not a word," Max said solemnly.

"Late at night, when the world is fast asleep and there's a fair chance that God is looking the other way ... I lie awake thinking up jokes."

"Where do you get your ideas?"

"You never know when an idea will hit you," replied the rabbi. "Trouble is, often an idea hits me at the most inappropriate time, when I'm supposed to be deadly serious. I'll give you an example, one that happened right here in Steelton. You recall, Maximilian, last October ... the day before Yom Kippur ... I led a small group of people to the St. Anne River for the ritual of emptying our pockets of sins. And Mr. Pripchik accidentally dropped a ten-dollar bill into the water — "

"And you almost drowned fishing it out?"

"Well, next day, Yom Kippur, just as the fast was coming to an end at sundown, and I was about to blow the shofar, it happened. I couldn't help it, Max. This joke just appeared — click! — like a test pattern on the television. There I am, you see, on a river bank, preaching this sermon about how we have to improve our ways in the new year ahead. And I'm in the middle of it when poor old Pripchik drops his tenspot in the river. And as I jump into the water to pluck it out, I'm saying 'We must alter our lives, my friends; it's a time for change.' And old Pripchik calls out: 'If it's all the same to you, Rabbi, I'll take two fives.' " Max nodded appreciatively, as if he and the rabbi were a couple of professionals trading anecdotes. "Now then, Mr. Glick, you may or may not think much of that joke, but at the time it nearly killed me. I knew it was going to be quite impossible for me to keep a straight face in front of the whole congregation. I made it through the blowing of the shofar ... thank God! ... and then I did the only thing I could do under the circumstances: I pretended to faint.

Can you imagine what my grandfather, my father, my older brother, and my uncles would do if they heard about that? There'd be a national week of mourning!"

"Do you think you'll be a comedy writer someday," Maximilian asked, "or will you always be a Lubavitcher rabbi?"

The rabbi shook his head slowly from side to side. "Who knows, Maximilian, what the next month, or the next day, or even the next minute, will bring? There isn't a person alive who can guarantee positively what will happen to you and me the moment I finish speaking this very sentence. In less time than it takes to blink, something happens to change a person's life. A phone rings and a man learns he has just won a lottery and is a millionaire. On the way to collect his winnings he falls down an open sewer and breaks both legs. A person can plan and plan, but no matter how much, how carefully you plan, there's always that spinning wheel — or that open sewer."

"Then why bother?" Maximilian wanted to know.

"Why bother!" The question astounded the Lubavitcher. "I'll tell you why, Mr. Glick. Because you're alive ... *alive*! You wanna lie down and die? Right here? Right now?"

"No," Maximilian responded hastily. Not only did Maximilian not want to die; he particularly didn't want to die on a wooden folding chair, with his last view of the world consisting of the interior of the Lubavitcher's chambers.

"The gift of life, Mr. Glick ... the gift of life! We're not talking here about Kleenex or orange peels. You just don't throw it away. There's always *hope*, you see."

A long sigh, at least twice his age, issued from Maximilian Glick. "Sometimes I wonder," he said.

Sensing his pupil's need to speak of some inner feeling, Rabbi Teitelman made a point of saying nothing, fearing that to encourage the boy to speak freely might drive him into silence.

Hesitantly, Max looked up at the rabbi. "If I tell *you* a secret, Rabbi — "

"Will I promise to keep my mouth shut, is that what you

want to know?" The Lubavitcher closed an imaginary zipper across his lips.

Max deliberated for a moment. Should he or shouldn't he?

Then slowly the boy's secret began to unfold. "There's this girl ... her name is Celia Brzjinski. ..." Briefly, simply, Maximilian told of his first meeting with Celia at the Blackthorns', of their involvement with one another, an involvement that began musically and grew during social hours spent with their piano teacher and his wife. He told of long leisurely walks home, friendly arguments: he thought memorizing Canadian poetry was the stupidest thing kids had to do at school; she thought memorizing the average rainfall and temperature of places like Kenya was stupider; London was the city she most wanted to visit (thanks to Derek Blackthorn's affectionate descriptions); Max chose Hong Kong, where the streets teemed with spies and fugitives — and people filming movies about spies and fugitives. Both agreed that the world's greatest pizza was definitely at Frank Senior's Pizzeria and that Morton Kelly, Steelton's foremost gourmand and food critic, was out of his skull insisting that the frozen stuff his mother bought at a supermarket had more mozzarella and pepperoni.

Rabbi Teitelman listened, nodding from time to time to indicate rapt attention. He winced a little at the thought of his pupil gorging himself on un-kosher pizza, compounding this crime by mixing dairy and meat products, but otherwise he displayed no reaction. "I don't get it, Max," he said when Max had finished. "What's the big secret? I think it's very admirable that the two of you have established ... uh ... what'll we call it? ... a professional working relationship."

Maximilian dropped his eyes. And it was then that the Lubavitcher understood Maximilian Glick's secret: he was in love.

The rabbi frowned, leaned forward, opened his desk drawer, and pretended to fumble for something. In fact, his eyes were already scanning the short list of Jewish families in Steelton. By now he had learned the names thoroughly; still, he wanted to be sure. Closing the drawer, Rabbi Teitelman sat back and looked at his unhappy pupil. "I think I'm beginning to understand, Max. When your name is Glick, a girl by the name of Brzjinski is definitely from the wrong side of the tracks, even though she lives only a few blocks away. Right?"

Max nodded. His shoulders drooped as if he were carrying suitcases packed with troubles.

"How do the folks at home feel about this?" the rabbi asked.

"I haven't told them. Not a peep. They'd turn into hydrogen bombs if they found out. That's all I ever hear at home ... how someday I'm going to be a brain surgeon, a judge, and a famous scientist all at the same time, plus entertain thousands of friends at the piano. And I'm going to marry a Jewish girl who is also a brain surgeon, a judge, a famous scientist, and entertains thousands of friends at the piano!"

"And your plans are what?" asked Rabbi Teitelman.

"To go to New York some day ... Celia and I, that is ... and study at Juilliard. And then ... I'm not sure if it'll be 'The Two-Piano Team of Glick and Brzjinski' or 'Brzjinski and Glick.' Which do you think sounds better?"

"Do I have to make a snap judgment?" asked the rabbi.

"No."

"Then I'd like to think about it, Max."

There was a long pause. "I've got a problem, haven't I?" the boy said at last.

The rabbi hedged. "You're still very young Max — "

"I'll be thirteen soon," Maximilian said gravely.

Teitelman chuckled. "Thirteen! My God, Glick, I hope you haven't neglected to make your will!" No sooner had Rabbi Teitelman uttered this quip than he knew he'd said the wrong thing at the wrong time. "I'm sorry, Max; I didn't mean to poke fun. All I meant was ... well, it's very important for a man of twelve to keep his options open — "

"Options? — "

"Your choices in life. You're a very lucky young man, my friend. You have so much going for you ... youth, good health, a family that cares deeply about you, and you're not exactly the stupidest kid I ever met, I'm forced to admit."

"Rabbi Kaminsky's daughter . . . her name was Rita . . . *she* had a lot of things going for her too. But when she chose a husband her parents didn't approve of, they treated her like she'd died or something."

"I know the story of Rita Kaminsky, Max. But she was considerably older than you when all that happened."

"But it could happen to me, too, couldn't it? Not at twelve, maybe, but how about when I'm, say, twenty-four?"

Rabbi Teitelman studied his young pupil, pondering the most painless way to respond. "Max. . . ." There was, he decided, no painless way. "Max, ambitions like yours can't be hidden under mattresses, or at the back of a drawerful of socks. You make decisions, and you have to live with those decisions. I only hope that you'll remember what I said a moment ago . . . if you are blessed with options, you must keep them as open as possible, for as long as possible."

Despite the Lubavitcher's sympathetic tone, it was a cheerless response. "I'm sorry if I've depressed you," said Teitelman. "There's an old saying, Max: he who would rest on truth lies down on a bed of nails."

"Who said that?"

"*I* did."

The rabbi glanced at his watch. "Hey, Glick," he said, "we've gone into overtime. One of us better get paid extra for this."

He rose, doffed his skullcap, and plunked the oversize black hat with the wide brim squarely on his head. "I'm off to Kerkorian's for a dozen eggs," he said. "You happen to be heading in that direction, Maximilian?" he added casually.

Wheels turned in the boy's brain. Across an imaginary screen, "Yes" suddenly appeared. "As a matter of fact, I am."

"Good," said Rabbi Teitelman, "we'll walk together."

As the boy and the Lubavitcher rabbi slogged along at a steady pace, their winter boots ploughing the slush like ships' prows, the rabbi shivered. "Next time God calls me to a community, I hope it's in southern California. Florida would do, too," he said.

"Why do you say 'next time'?" Max asked.

"Because we never know, do we? Spinning wheels and open sewers, Mr. Glick, remember?"

All the expected evening faces were on the street, their eyes darting from Max to the oddity walking by his side. Max knew what they were thinking. There was the occasional "Hello" or "Hi there" or a simple nod of greeting and recognition, but Max could feel people's heads turning as they passed, staring at this pair, and especially at the strange-looking clergyman. And sure enough, the bakery bunch were at their customary lookout, taking careful note.

They continued heading east on King Street in the direction of Kerkorian's, one of the last corner grocery stores in a world of supermarkets. They entered the store, stamping their feet, inhaling the friendly, clean aroma of the place — a heady mixture of spice, citrus, soaps of all kinds. The owner, Amos Kerkorian, was standing as always near the front door behind his cash register, in shirtsleeves, bald head covered with an old shapeless Donegal tweed cap, paunch protected behind a white apron tied with a huge bow at the back. It seemed to Maximilian that Kerkorian spent his life in those same clothes behind that same cash register; that he ate there, slept there, raised his family there, and would probably die there.

Anyone hoping to enter and leave Kerkorian's anonymously hoped in vain. The grocer's voice was a trumpet that blasted greetings across the length and breadth of his store like a fanfare. "Hello hello hello!" he shouted over his ancient cash register. "It's Rabbi Teitelman, and Maestro Glick!" There were three or four customers in the store, all of whom promptly abandoned their shopping baskets and lists to fasten their eyes on the Lubavitcher and his pupil. "To what do I owe the honor?" asked Kerkorian.

"To the fact that I need a dozen eggs," the rabbi responded.

"One dozen of our finest Grade A's, coming up!" To Max the grocer said: "And what can I do for you, Maestro?"

"I'll ... uh ... I'll just have — " Max fumbled awkwardly. How could he admit he'd only come along because, for the first time, he wanted to be in the Lubavitcher's company?

"He's my bodyguard," explained Rabbi Teitelman, coming to Maximilian's rescue.

An outspoken man, Kerkorian said: "Lemme tell you something, Rabbi . . . no offence meant, of course. If you don't start eating something besides eggs all the time, you ain't gonna have a body to guard. Know what you need? A Grade A wife."

From the other customers came discreet titters. Conscious that he was the center of attention, Rabbi Teitelman calmly brought the discussion of his marital status to a close. "I'm very grateful for your concern, Mr. Kerkorian. Someday God may be kind enough to send me a wife. Until He does, I'll have to be content to share my home with a dozen eggs."

Good, thought Maximilian, that settles that; now let's just get the eggs and get out of here. Unlike Rabbi Teitelman, who accepted Kerkorian's bold suggestions as well as the stares of the other customers with good grace, Max was becoming increasingly uncomfortable. He wanted to cry out to the other customers: "What are you all gawking at? We're not a circus act!" It seemed as though Kerkorian was taking forever to slip the carton of eggs into a bag, to ring up the sale, to count out the change.

At last, Rabbi Teitelman and the boy turned to leave.

"Oh-oh!" Amos Kerkorian said in a loud whisper. "Look who's coming. . . . Mister Pain-in-the-neck himself."

The front door of the shop opened just as the shopkeeper spoke these words of warning, and Maximilian recognized the one man he did *not* want to see at this point.

Maximilian's dread was contagious. Rabbi Teitelman took a deep breath, then out of the side of his mouth whispered to his pupil: "Pray for courage Maximilian . . . *courage!*"

12

The man closing the shop door behind him, stamping the slush from his overshoes, clapping his gloved hands together to generate warmth in them, was Morris Moskover, the Local Sage.

With forced courtesy, Kerkorian called out: "Hello Mr. Moskover."

"Kerkorian my friend," said Moskover, "you ready to do some serious business?"

Kerkorian cast his eyes toward the heavens, asking for strength. "What can I do for you tonight, Mr. Moskover?" he asked patiently.

"I'd like a nice piece of Swiss cheese. A pound will do." Moskover wagged a gloved finger at the grocer. "*Nice*, mind you."

"Would I sell you Swiss cheese that *wasn't* nice?" said the grocer, insulted.

"You know how Swiss cheese is, Kerkorian," said Moskover. "Sometimes the holes aren't right, especially when they're too big. And, of course, when they're too small it's no good either, is it? I want holes that aren't too big . . . or too small."

"You want to buy a pound of cheese or a pound of holes?" Kerkorian demanded, his patience now leaking away quickly.

Moskover laughed. "Kerkorian, it's a lucky thing for you that I'm a believer in loyalty. Everybody says 'Moskover, you're out of your mind, you should shop at the supermarkets, they got everything, and cheaper too!'. . . but good old Morris

Moskover says 'Nossiree, I been Amos Kerkorian's valuable and true customer for thirty long years!'"

"Maybe it's time you started taking everybody's advice," said Kerkorian, reaching wearily for a slab of Swiss cheese the size of a concrete block.

It was only after this exchange that the eyes of Morris Moskover fell upon Rabbi Teitelman and Maximilian standing off to one side, both teacher and pupil hoping to escape unnoticed. But no such luck. The eyes of Morris Moskover were small piercing eyes capable of seeing under carpets and behind closed doors — any place where there was something that was none of their business. In Moskover's long narrow face were deep lines which the raw January winds etched deeper and which, when he laughed, became deeper again, almost sinister. A man who regularly dispensed advice to others at the drop of a hat, Moskover regarded himself as an expert on everything from buttering bread to manufacturing space rockets. His own business — he had once owned a clothing store — had gone bankrupt so many times over the years that his creditors had lost count. Nobody was quite sure how he and his wife now supported themselves, but it was a good bet they were living off the kindness of a son-in-law, a professional gambler in Chicago.

"Tell me, young fella," Moskover said, after greeting the rabbi and Maximilian, "you still taking piano lessons from that stretched-out noodle, what's-his-name — "

"Mr. Blackthorn — "

"Yeah, Barrack Blackthorn," said Moskover.

"It's Derek . . ." the boy corrected him. "D-E-R-E-K — "

"Derek, Barrack — what's it matter? If you ask me, they're a coupla spies."

"Who are?" Max asked.

"Barrack Blackthorn and that Madame Butterfly he lives with. The one they call Suzuki."

"Shizuko," Max interjected.

"Shizuko, Suzuki — what's it matter? It's all the same."

"What makes you think they're spies?" Rabbi Teitelman asked Moskover.

"You ever seen a couple like that before?" Moskover said, narrowing his beady eyes.

"No," the rabbi admitted.

"Then that proves it," said Moskover.

"What country do you figure they're spies for?" asked the rabbi, pretending to take Moskover seriously.

"Ach, what's it matter? A spy's a spy, and that's all there is to it. It's certainly not a business normal decent human beings go into."

Once again Moskover turned his attention to Maximilian. "Tell me, young fella — " Morris Moskover always seemed to begin his sentences with those very words, making the boy feel as if he were on trial before some Lord High Executioner. "Tell me. . . . The old man, your grandfather I mean, says you're gonna be a judge when you grow up. Lemme give you a piece of advice, my young friend. You be a furniture-man like your father and your grandfather. In my whole life I never bought five cents worth of anything from a judge. But furniture? Hmph. Millions I've spent! Just a coupla weeks ago the Missus complains to me, 'Morris, the chesterfield's no good any more, I can't find a comfortable spot to sit.' I tell her we've had that chesterfield thirty years and better she should go on a diet and lose fifty pounds. You think I didn't end up buying a new sofa at Glick's? Cost me an arm and a leg. Something else to remember, boy. Never marry a woman with fancy ideas!"

Maximilian opened his mouth, but a quick nod from Rabbi Teitelman told him not to bother. Better to let the Local Sage rave on.

"Anyway, there's one thing I'm glad about, Maxie," said Moskover.

"What's that?"

"I'm glad the old man says this music business is only a sideline with you. Listen to me, young fella, in the village I came from in Russia, you know how musicians lived? Like crows, eating seeds off the roads."

Again Maximilian was tempted to argue but before he could get a word out Rabbi Teitelman had noisily cleared his throat.

"You're quite right," said the rabbi to Moskover. "Music should be a person's hobby, nothing else." The rabbi shot his pupil a stern look. "Isn't that so, Maximilian?"

"Uh, yes . . . yes, that's so," Maximilian said.

Relishing his own wisdom, Moskover rocked on his heels, hands folded across his stomach. "Well, I'm certainly glad to hear you say that, Maxie. Wouldn't want to see a young fella in this day and age playing for his dinner on some street corner."

Moskover diverted his attention momentarily to the scale where Amos Kerkorian was weighing the piece of cheese. "Make sure it's a pound," he cautioned, again with a wag of his index finger.

"As a matter of fact, it's eighteen ounces," said Kerkorian, barely managing to hold his temper, "but I'll only charge you for a pound."

To the rabbi Moskover now said: "Did I tell you I been a steady customer here for thirty years?"

"Yes you did," Teitelman replied respectfully. "That's a long time."

"Well, Rabbi," said Moskover, becoming mellow, "I'm one of the oldest Jewish settlers in Steelton. I came here over fifty years ago, long before you were born. How old d'ya think I am?"

The rabbi shrugged. "I don't know." Secretly he figured well over eighty.

"Seventy-seven!" Moskover shouted proudly, as if he had just captured seventy-seven enemy soldiers singlehandedly.

Rabbi Teitelman offered the only honest thing he could. "You certainly don't look your age." Moskover of course chose to take this as a compliment. "Of course I look a lot younger. Know why? Because I, Morris Moskover, hold the magic formula for eternal youth!"

Everyone in the store, including Amos Kerkorian, focused their attention on the Sage.

"What," asked Rabbi Teitelman, "is the magic formula, Mr. Moskover?"

"A sense of humor, Rabbi. A sense of *humor!*"

Looking even more serious and respectful, the Lubavitcher said: "You are indeed a blessed man, Mr. Moskover."

Moskover agreed fully. "I'll tell the world I'm a blessed man!" Then he began in a quiet confidential tone: "Mind if I give you a friendly piece of advice, Rabbi? I mean I'm old enough to be your father, even though I don't look it." His eyes, like rivets, fastened themselves in the Lubavitcher's pale face. "What you need, Rabbi . . . is to develop a sense of humor."

"Really?" The Lubavitcher displayed keen interest.

"Look, Rabbi, I like to come right to the point. That's Morris Moskover's way. I don't twist; I don't turn; I don't go in circles like most folks. If there's a problem, a person can always come to Morris Moskover for a solution. I have what's called an analytical mind, you see. An analytical mind, plus a sense of humor . . . the two go hand in hand. Do you understand what I'm saying?"

"Yes, yes I think so."

"Excellent! Then already you've made the first important step: you're *ready, willing,* and *able* to be helped by Morris Moskover. Now I come right to my point" — the Local Sage shook his head slowly from side to side, as if he'd caught the rabbi eating spareribs at Hong Ling's. "Last night, Rabbi . . . last night" — he shook his head again, more reproachfully. "Do you understand what I'm telling you, Rabbi?"

"You mean at the auditorium?"

Moskover lit up. "Ahah! You see now, don't you? That's how the analytical mind works, Rabbi. Now we're getting somewhere. That's Step Two. You wanna know Step Three?"

"By all means. Please go on," said the Lubavitcher.

"Step Three!" Moskover announced. Then, in an even more confidential tone: "Last night was what a man gifted with an analytical mind would call spilt milk. I have a knack for calling a spade a spade, and last night can only be described in one word — Spilt Milk. And you know what they say about spilt milk — "

Teitelman delayed his response long enough to thrust a hand into his trouser pocket and pinch himself. "I believe the expression is: Never cry over spilt milk."

"Straight to the head of the class!" cried Moskover. "You're beginning to follow my line of thinking, I can see that. The analytical mind ... logic ... everything in order, Step One, Step Two, Step Three. Ready for Step Four?"

Without sarcasm, but striving mightily not to laugh in the face of his new mentor, Teitelman said: "I can hardly wait."

"The fourth step is to think positive ... by which I mean that when a person such as yourself isn't blessed with a natural sense of humor, he's gotta make a point of working at it. Understand what I'm saying? You gotta *practise* it, same way young Glick here practises piano."

"A couple of hours a day ... is that what you suggest?" asked the rabbi.

"Exactly. You set aside, say, an hour before breakfast; another hour before bed. And you practise telling jokes, you read something funny you can use in your sermons, like for instance something from one of Buckner Finsterwald's stories. Do you understand what I'm saying, Rabbi?"

"Oh yes, yes indeed." Rabbi Teitelman took a firmer grip on his parcel of eggs, ready to leave. But Morris Moskover laid a restraining hand on him.

"One more thing, Rabbi. Call it Step Five. Timing. Timing!" he repeated. "Like the Good Book says, there's a time for everything. A time to be born, a time to die, a time to make jokes — " Moskover paused to gather moral force for the rest of the homily. "And a time *not* to make jokes!"

"You mean ..." Teitelman put in, "a sense of the fitness of things?"

With a curt wave of his hand, Moskover brushed away the rabbi's suggestion. "Why use a hundred words when one will do? Timing, that's what I'm talking about. Now take last night ... it was an occasion to do a lot of things. But to crack jokes?"

The young rabbi looked hastily about him. Kerkorian and

the other customers in the shop were all ears. Was *this*, he asked himself, what the Local Sage meant by timing?

"Do you really think" — Moskover was not about to let up — "last night was the proper time and place to try out a comedy act?"

As the supplier of local color, much of which had formed the basis of Teitelman's "invocation" the night before, Maximilian Glick felt that both he and his protégé (for that was how he now regarded Teitelman) were being impugned. If the Lubavitcher was not of a mind to defend his own performance, then Maximilian Glick, the rabbi's personal intelligence agent, would have to take up sword and shield for him. "Mr. Moskover," Max said, "that question's really not — "

"Max!" Teitelman cut in sharply. Then, softly, he said to his pupil: "It's okay, Max; relax ... *relax*." He returned to Moskover. "I'm beginning to appreciate how well you've earned your reputation in Steelton, Mr. Moskover."

Moskover shrugged. "Earned is an understatement, Rabbi. Believe me, more than one person in this town has said *I'm* the one the Governor General should give a medal to. Last night Zelig Peikes, and that tight-wad Milt Katzenberg, and the old man, Maxie's grandfather ... they were ready to do terrible things, *terrible* things. But I said to them: 'Gentlemen, be analytical, be logical, be positive!' Thank God there's one cool head in Steelton. Even Buckner Finsterwald himself, when he heard me reasoning with them, was full of praise. 'This man is a messiah!' That's what Buckner Finsterwald called me. And that's why I'm so glad you had the good fortune to run into me tonight, Rabbi. Better all this should come from a man of wisdom ... a man of humor. Do you understand what I'm saying?"

Teitelman tried to sound grateful. "It's not every day that a man gets advice like yours, Mr. Moskover."

"Good, good. I knew you'd take what I had to say in the proper spirit." Moskover gave the rabbi a fatherly pat on the shoulder, took up his small parcel of cheese, and turned to leave.

"Just a moment, Mr. Moskover," Amos Kerkorian piped up. "That'll be two dollars ninety-three cents, please."

"Put it on my account, Kerkorian," Moskover responded. "I have a big dividend cheque coming next week. My son-in-law from Chicago handles all my investments these days, you know. Pay you next Wednesday, for sure."

Kerkorian shook his head. "Sorry, Mr. Moskover, but no more credit."

Old Morris Moskover's jaw dropped, and Maximilian noticed that there was a darkish stubble on it, like tiny iron filings. Disbelief in his sharp little eyes, Moskover said: "I . . . I beg your pardon?"

"I said no more credit, Mr. Moskover. I got to pay for my merchandise when I buy it at the wholesale, and I got to get paid when I sell it to my customers. Simple as that." Kerkorian looked over toward the rabbi and Maximilian and winked slyly.

Moskover, meanwhile, was beside himself. "B-b-but . . . ," he sputtered.

Kerkorian held out his hand. "Cash, Mr. Moskover," he said in a very business-like manner. "Two dollars ninety-three cents, please."

Once again the other customers in the shop were all eyes and ears. Like a beetle pinned to the center of a display card, the Sage began to squirm. Beneath his thick overcoat his body shook, first with confusion, then annoyance, then anger. "I been your customer for thirty years, Kerkorian. For a rotten two dollars ninety-three cents you don't trust *me*, Morris Moskover? This is an outrage!" he screamed.

For a split second there was silence in the grocery store. Then Kerkorian threw back his head and burst into laughter. "Oh God, Mr. Moskover . . . oh God!"

"What's so funny?" Moskover's face was now ashen.

"I was. . . ." Again the grocer burst into laughter. "I was just kidding, for heaven's sake. It was just a joke."

"You call that a joke!"

"C'mon," said Kerkorian, "where's that famous sense of

humor of yours, Mr. Moskover? The sense of humor you were just talking about?"

"You call that a joke!" Moskover repeated. "Listen to me Kerkorian, I don't need your crummy credit. I got investments, you hear? Big investments . . . in Chicago. My son-in-law is a big important financial consultant in Chicago. He can buy and sell the likes of you just by snapping his fingers."

Kerkorian's face instantly turned as ashen as Moskover's. "Nobody can buy and sell Amos Kerkorian just by snapping fingers . . . nobody! And as for your fancy son-in-law in Chicago, the whole town knows he's really a gambler, a sharpie. I seen him here in Steelton a coupla years ago in his white Cadillac, with his foot-long cigar sticking outa his mouth. If *he's* a financial consultant, *I'm* the Queen of England!"

Moskover stepped forward to the counter and faced the grocer across the old brass cash register. "That remark will cost you thousands of dollars, Kerkorian. From now on I take my business to the supermarket!" He threw down the cheese — all eighteen ounces — and without so much as a nod in the direction of Rabbi Teitelman and Max, stormed out of the shop, slamming the door behind him with such force that the façade of the building shook and a pyramid of oranges in Kerkorian's window collapsed.

Back on the sidewalk once more, Maximilian and the rabbi walked together in stunned silence. The boy was now completely oblivious to other pedestrians or passing motorists. Whoever saw the pair together, or didn't — it didn't matter to Max. All he could think of were the strange events he'd just witnessed.

At last, after they'd walked a block, the boy stopped dead in his tracks.

"What is it, Maximilian?"

"I don't understand it — "

"Understand what?"

"I don't understand anything that happened in there. It's crazy!"

"No Maximilian," said the Lubavitcher, "it wasn't crazy.

At least, no crazier than life. You remember, I told you no-body can guarantee what will happen to people from one second to the next? God had a choice, you see. He could have made us into dull predictable animals. You know, jiggle a little bell and we come running for a banana. Or He could have made us into the kind of mystery packages that we are. And He chose, obviously, to populate the world with mystery packages ... you, me, Moskover, Kerkorian, and a few billion others. Open the wrapping, and God only knows what you'll find inside."

"But something's not right," Max protested. "All the time old Moskover was standing there, accusing you of not having a sense of humor, you said nothing, not a word. Why didn't you tell him?"

"Tell me," said the Lubavitcher, "if I'd told Morris Moskover the truth about myself ... or if *you* had told him ... which, thank God, you didn't! ... would Morris Moskover have un-derstood?"

Maximilian pondered the question. "No," he said at last, "no, he wouldn't have understood. But all the same I sure had an urge to tell him how wrong he was."

"Still, Maximilian, you chose to hold your tongue."

"A secret's a secret."

"Yes," said the Lubavitcher. "And don't feel bad about me. What's more important — much more important — is what you learned in there. The difference between a fool and a sage, a *real* sage, is that the sage knows when to keep quiet. And now you'd better head for home or your folks'll think you're being held prisoner in some Lubavitcher dun-geon. Goodnight Mr. Glick."

They parted at a street corner, Max starting north toward Pine Hill, the rabbi west to his small apartment. Suddenly Max swung round. "Rabbi," he called back, "Rabbi...." Teitelman turned. "Yes, Maximilian?"

The boy walked back to where the rabbi was standing. "I was wondering...."

"Yes?"

"I was wondering — uh — well, I know you have very strict rules about food and what you can eat and what you can't. But I — uh — "

"Well, out with it, Mr. Glick. Otherwise they're gonna have to chop us out of the ice in the morning." The rabbi pretended to be freezing to death.

"Do you think, if we're careful about what we serve ... you could come for supper at our house one night next week?"

The young Lubavitcher's pale face grew very stern. "I must warn you, Mr. Glick, I'm a fearsome guest."

"Fearsome?"

"Yes, a terror. I run my fingers over furniture to check for dust; I inspect the insides of refrigerators and stoves. I do chemical tests on the wine and food — "

"Will you come for supper one night?"

"Invite me, and I'll come."

The first announcement Maximilian made when he entered the house on Pine Hill was, "Guess who's coming to supper one night soon ... the rabbi!"

Sarah Glick dropped her soup ladle, Henry Glick dropped his evening paper, and both cried out at the same time.

"Good grief!" Sarah Glick then said quietly as she sat down slowly on a kitchen stool. "What do you serve to a man like that? Air and water?"

"You ever tried making the world's largest omelette?" said her husband.

Both father and mother Glick stared at their son. Still quiet, as if resigned to catastrophe, Sarah Glick said to Maximilian: "What have you gone and done?"

The boy smiled at his mother.

Then he remembered Rabbi Teitelman's words: the spinning wheel ... the open sewer....

And the boy's smile vanished. "I'm not sure," he said.

13

Five o'clock on a dark February afternoon, at the intersection of King and Queen streets. All three regulation catastrophes are present: dead-center lies a sewer excavation of archaeological proportions, freshly dug by the Steelton Works Department (out-of-season, unaccountably). The traffic lights are out of order; as a further act of public mischief they flash green for all directions. Enticed by green lights everywhere, but frustrated by striped wooden barricades and piles of freezing mud, motorists improvise their way out of no-man's land, some cavalierly mounting curbs and transforming sidewalks into bypasses, others executing bold U-turns and backups. They shout at each other through half-open steamy windows, swelling the wintry dusk with a chorale of angry advice. A lone police officer, Corporal Wilson (recently promoted from Constable First Class), dispatched to restore order, drops his arms to his sides. His whistle dangles in silence at the end of its cord. Someday, in retirement, sitting by a crackling fire, he will tell his grandchildren of days like this. He will tell them how he stood his ground. He will omit the sad fact of his defeat.

Add to these catastrophes a fourth: a van has just broken down near the rim of the excavation. The blockage complete, all traffic now comes to a tangled standstill.

The stalled van is the type used by campers and sportsmen, with a wide sliding side door and double doors at the rear. It is all black, severely black, not a speck of trim anywhere. So clogged with ice and snow are the wheel-wells that the tires appear locked in place. Except for two fan-shaped clearings in the windshield where the wipers have done some good, the van is coated with a thick layer of road-salt and dirt. From top to bottom the vehicle is a mess. Wherever it has come from — a battlefield? a swamp? — it has blazed its own trail.

A bronchial cough comes from the engine compartment as the driver attempts to start the motor; it seems the van's trouble is respiratory. On the curb, a few steps away, Cal Irwin, the hardware dealer, officially informs a knot of curious pedestrians: "She's either gettin' too much air, or not enough, that's for sure." Fancying himself an expert, he cups his hands around his mouth and through this megaphone calls to the unseen operator of the van: "She's flooded for godsake. Press the gas pedal to the floor and start 'er up. Press it right to the floor." Someday, in *his* retirement, Irwin will tell his grandchildren how one January day he saved the hour at King and Queen.

The operator, still invisible, follows Irwin's instructions. The van sputters into half-life, for a few seconds convulses, then whimpers and dies.

"Oh for godsake," mutters Irwin, feeling superior to whatever idiot sits behind the wheel of the van. He then steps manfully off the curb, ignoring the ankle-deep slush into which his low boots have disappeared, and plants himself directly in front of the van, the better to repeat his expert recommendations to the driver. Drawing so close that his nose nearly rubs the windshield, he peers inside.

"For godsake!" he exclaims again.

Suddenly the driver's side window comes down and a young man sticks his head out. "That's three times you've mentioned the Lord's name. Maybe you can tell us if He's provided a Ford dealer in these parts?"

Irwin stares at the driver, blinks, stares again. So full of command only moments earlier, he now stands speechless, his tongue as immobile as the black van.

The other side window is lowered and the front-seat passenger pokes his head out. "It's Moscow all right," he says to the driver. "I *told* you we shoulda turned right at Grand Rapids."

"Impossible," scoffs the driver. "Moscow's not this cold."

By this time a crowd has formed around Irwin at the front of the van as irate motorists abandon their cars to investigate the hold-up. "Holy Mother!" whispers one of the onlookers, almost in awe. "There's *two* of 'em."

Another whispers: "They look like that rabbi fellow ... the weird-looking one with the — "

"Shhh!" hisses a third, as if the mere mention of the Lubavitcher will turn everyone within range into pillars of salt.

Now the wide side door of the van slides open and two more young men emerge. Like the driver and the front-seat passenger, they are dressed in black wide-brimmed hats and long black coats, they wear thick beards and sidelocks; they stretch, then begin vigorously to clap their gloved hands.

"They seem to be applauding. Must be some kind of ritual," observes a woman in the crowd. "That sort usually have strange customs," explains her companion.

One of the handclappers blows warm breath onto his gloves. "It's definitely some kind of ritual," insists the woman.

The driver climbs down from behind the wheel. "Has anybody seen my blood anywhere?" he calls out to no one in particular, flapping his arms about him wildly to restore circulation. His passenger, also climbing down, replies: "You must've left it back in Detroit." He too engages in strenuous arm-flapping.

The driver speaks again to Cal Irwin: "Is there a service station nearby?"

Irwin's self-confidence returns. "No need for that," he huffs. "Here, allow me — " He slips behind the wheel of the van and turns the ignition key. From the engine compartment comes the slow low grinding of a motor earnestly attempting to revive. Seizing the moment, Irwin slams the accelerator to the floor.

"This'll clear her," he assures the driver. The grinding grows slower, lower. Then silence. Dead.

"I better open the hood," says the van driver.

Cal Irwin, facing public disgrace, clings to the wheel, as if waiting for Fate to vindicate his judgment. "She's flooded. Nothing more."

The driver opens the hood, bends, and peers into the engine's tomb.

Cal Irwin winks at acquaintances in the crowd and calls to the driver: "You got any idea at all what you're lookin' at under there?"

"Well," replies the driver slowly, "for one thing, I'm looking at a loose distributor cap, so I don't suppose there's much point removing the air cleaner to check the carburetor."

Corporal Wilson has now made his way through the crowd. "What's the trouble here?" he asks in a voice that matches his six-foot-six frame.

"She's flooded, Ernie, that's all," Irwin tells the policeman.

"I heard something about a loose distributor cap," says the Corporal.

"It's more likely the starting system," says the driver. "I had a problem with the ring gear coupla weeks ago."

"She gettin' any spark?" Corporal Wilson asks.

"Not much," the driver confesses, "but I've tightened up the distributor cap."

"Start 'er up, Cal, "the Corporal orders.

"Roger," Irwin responds, supporting the Law to the hilt. The engine remains lifeless. "She's flooded all right," says Irwin, "and that's final."

"Then we better get 'er outa here for starters," Wilson decides.

"Got any good ideas?" the van driver asks him.

Wilson takes long strides toward the rear of the van, its four occupants trailing after him. "A strong back's better than a good idea," he says. His manner is laconic. The shoulder he presses against the rear doors of the van is as broad as a cow's rump. On either side of him the black-clad travelers arrange themselves, like a quartet of pallbearers. "Okay," says Wilson, "heave!" They strain, they grunt. The feet of one give way on the slippery road and he ends up on his knees. "Again," Wilson barks, *"heave!"*

But the van seems rooted to the roadway, perhaps forever.

"One more time," Corporal Wilson says. But the quartet's attention is no longer on him, as in disbelief they watch a young man, wearing attire similar to theirs, advancing through the bystanders.

"I don't believe my eyes," says the van driver.

"Hi there," calls the man approaching.

The driver laughs. "You the local Ford dealer?"

"How'd you guess? Name's Teitelman, Kalman Teitelman. Welcome to Steelton."

"I'm Reuben Calish," says the driver. His three fellow-travelers desert their post at the rear of the van and come forward, brushing road-salt from their black coats, leaving Corporal Wilson to survey his second major defeat of the day. "Say hello to Corey Silverstone, Manny Kirsch, and Horrible Herman Hitzik, so called because he gets car-sick even when we aren't moving."

"Welcome to Steelton," Teitelman repeats. "I'm the rabbi here."

"Rabbi!" says Horrible Herman Hitzik, astounded. "You mean they have *Jews* here?"

"Where there's oxygen there's Jews," says Teitelman smiling. "Where you all from?"

"Detroit . . . Michigan," says Calish.

Teitelman laughs. "I know Detroit's in Michigan. I'm from Boston . . . *Massachusetts,* that is. Who's the guy behind the wheel?"

Hearing this question, Cal Irwin leans out the van window. "I'm Cal Irwin . . . Irwin's Hardware. We're not together. I'm just tryin' to help out. She's flooded."

Corporal Wilson rejoins them. "Evening, Reverend," he nods to Rabbi Teitelman. "These here friends of yours?"

Reuben Calish, besides being the driver of the van, seems

to be the spokesman for its crew. "You better say yes to the officer," he tells Teitelman. "I think we're already in big trouble here." To Corporal Wilson he says, in a serious vein, "How can we get hold of a tow-truck?"

"You don't need a tow-truck, I tell ya," Cal Irwin, who has welded himself to the steering wheel of the van, says stubbornly. "Give 'er another minute or two to drain and I'll have 'er going. Matter of fact, she's probably clear enough now —"

Calish is about to caution Irwin not to try again, but it's too late. From some hidden resource deep within the bowels of the vehicle, a spark of life finds its way into the engine, barely adequate to create the familiar grinding noise. Despite the cold, Irwin has removed his hat and, hand twisting the ignition key as if squeezing out its last drop of blood, he sweats and curses quietly.

"You're killing 'er for sure," warns Corporal Wilson.

"I'm *not*, Ernie," Irwin insists.

"I'm afraid you are," says Calish, no longer worried about appearing ungrateful.

"Better leave off, Cal," Wilson says.

The grinding noise goes on, like a death rattle.

Calish looks over at Teitelman and shrugs the kind of shrug that asks "What are we going to do with this fellow?" Teitelman shrugs the kind of shrug that answers "God only knows."

Then, for no reason at all, Rabbi Teitelman extends a foot and kicks the right front tire of the van.

As if struck by lightning, the engine explodes into a roar. There is a sudden acrid cloud of smoke that envelops the van and all who surround it. When the smoke clears, Irwin can be seen grinning proudly behind the wheel. "Didn't I tell ya!" he exults.

Two women standing behind Rabbi Teitelman — the two who were a few minutes earlier convinced that they were witnessing tribal rites — now begin whispering intently with other onlookers. Faces become half-invisible as their words, issued into the below-zero air, turn into clouds of steam.

"Did *you* see that? *I* saw it. I swear, that's all he did, he just kicked the right front tire —"

"They say that's how he got rid of the bank robbers ... same way. . . . Must have some special kind of power."

"Weird, weird, that's what I call it."

"Didn't I tell ya!" Irwin calls out to the crowd, still rejoicing in what he takes to be his own triumph.

Corporal Wilson's square jaw widens into a half-smile, as if he is half-willing to admit to witnessing a miracle. "It was the Reverend here that got 'er started, Cal. Not you."

Feeling injured, Cal Irwin gives up the driver's seat. "If there's one thing I know, it's cars," he mutters to the policeman.

"Maybe you know cars," Corporal Wilson replies, "but the Reverend here ... he knows somebody higher up."

Reuben Calish offers his hand to Cal Irwin. "You were a great help," he says graciously. They shake hands, but Irwin is surly. But for the accidental kicking of a tire by a rabbinical foot, the moment would have been his.

"C'mon," Calish calls to his fellow-travelers, "we better clear out of here." He thanks Corporal Wilson who responds with an informal salute. "Can we give you a lift somewhere?" he asks Rabbi Teitelman.

"Sure. You can drive me home. We'll have tea."

"Great. Hop in."

The crowd disperses, some shaking their heads, some laughing. Minus the stalled van, the chaos at King and Queen continues, Corporal Wilson still blowing his one-note repertoire on his whistle.

From his compact kitchenette, where he is making tea, Teitelman calls to his fellow Lubavitchers: "It's not the Waldorf Astoria, but it's burglar-proof ... not that there's anything to steal."

"The main thing is, it's warm!" says Manny Kirsch. He is busily massaging the cold from his limbs.

"The main thing," says Horrible Herman Hitzik, "is that it's stationary!"

Over tea, which they drink boiling hot with much lip-smacking and groans of relief, Calish and his friends explain their current mission. Their van is referred to in Lubavitch circles as a "Mitzva-mobile" — a rolling tabernacle filled with traditional Orthodox paraphernalia of prayer: a stack of book-lets of scripture, neatly folded white satin prayer shawls with blue bands at the borders and long stringy fringes, small velvet pouches containing sets of phylacteries, boxes of literature about the Lubavitch movement. The Mitzva-mobile (or "good-work" mobile) belongs to the Lubavitch community of Detroit. Its customary territory is a busy street corner in a suburb of Detroit heavily populated with Jews. On fair days, and even foul, the Mitzva-mobile can be found at its station, its rotating crews standing by its open doors on the sidewalk, examining the faces of passersby for those barely perceptible signals — the twitch of a lip, perhaps, or the slight rise of an eyebrow — for anything that says: "Ah, here's a candidate . . . someone who's ready to travel *our* highway back to Heaven."

"You're about four hundred miles north of your usual street corner," Kalman Teitelman notes.

"We're on our way to Ottawa," says Calish. "You see, the four of us are also entertainers, so we often get invitations to perform for other Lubavitch communities. Usually they're close to Detroit . . . you know, cities in Lower Michigan, Illinois, Indiana. Ottawa's the farthest we've ever traveled."

"Don't count your chickens before they're hatched," says Hitzik. "At the rate we're going, we may never see civilization again."

Calish is an accordion player, Corey Silverstone a clari-netist, and Manny Kirsch a drummer. "Hitzik sings," Calish explains, "when he's not car-sick."

"We better get started," says Hitzik, without relish. He glances at his wristwatch. "We're already way behind schedule."

Teitelman says: "There's no way you'll make it to Ottawa tonight. It's hundreds of miles away. The nearest town is Nickel City and, frankly, from what the Steeltonites say of it, Nickel City is Sodom and Gomorrah all wrapped into one. I suggest you spend the night here. My abode is humble, but it's better than being found frozen to death on Highway 17. There's only one problem ... supper. I'm supposed to be dining out tonight ... at the Glicks' ... they're members of my congregation. I'll call and cancel. Then I'll pick up some groceries and we'll have ourselves a kosher pig-out. Okay?"

His unexpected guests insist that he keep his social engagement, but Teitelman is adamant. On the telephone to Sarah Glick he is profoundly apologetic. "I *do* hope you understand, Mrs. Glick. ... I know it's last-minute, but if I could please have a raincheck —"

Sarah Glick is firm. "You *must* bring your friends," she insists graciously. As she says these words, she grimaces at Maximilian, hoping there's enough to accommodate four extra hungry men. "I'm sorry," she says in a motherly tone to the rabbi, "I simply will *not* take no for an answer. There's plenty for everybody...."

In the Glick diningroom, a second Miracle of the Fishes has occurred, but this time they are smoked fishes, imported along with several kinds of cheese from a market in Toronto whose kosher standards are high enough to merit the Lubavitcher rabbi's approval.

Similarly, two loaves of challah, baked for the occasion by Bryna Glick, have stretched wondrously among the hungered and road-weary guests from Detroit, Rabbi Teitelman, and five Glicks. Reuben Calish declares that the homemade bread is the best he's ever eaten. Bryna Glick points out that this is because she baked the challah in Sarah Glick's oven. She is openly resentful of the fact that the old oven fell into her daughter-in-law's hands when the house on Pine Hill passed to Henry and Sarah. "That stove has fed three generations of Glicks," she boasts to the visitors. Sarah Glick points out that it is also feeding three generations of Hendersons, Ned Henderson being the local electrician whose housecalls to repair the doddering appliance have recently increased from monthly to weekly. Sarah is thinking of trading it in for a sleek range full of dials and automatic devices. Hearing this, Bryna Glick threatens to repossess "my stove."

"Where on earth will you keep it?" Sarah says. "With all due respect, you've already got a stove in your apartment."

"In our bedroom," says Bryna Glick defiantly.

Henry Glick says to his wife and mother: "Why don't you two girls step outside and settle this?"

"Because it's too cold out there, that's why," says Bryna Glick. "Besides, Sarah and I aren't quarreling, we're merely discussing . . . isn't that so, Sarah dear?"

Remembering as always that there will be other sunrises, other battlepoints, Sarah Glick, flushed with annoyance, manages nevertheless to smile back.

"Peace!" cries Augustus Glick. He rises, his cheeks red from the effects of the first round of drinks, and begins to move about the table with a second bottle of brandy. Sarah and Bryna clap determined hands over their glasses, the men at the table extend theirs, and Augustus pours generously, as if the stuff flows from a bottomless well. "L'chayim, good health!" he cries, downs his portion in a single gulp, then growls rawly with satisfaction. The other men follow suit, throwing back their drinks with a quick turn of the wrist, gasping in pleasant agony as the liquor sends flames into their chests.

Coughing and chuckling, Augustus looks across the table to his grandson. "You see, Maximilian my boy, this is how *men* do it!"

"You mean, when I'm thirteen I have to be able to knock it back like that?" Max asks.

"Good God no!" says Sarah Glick, her eyes shooting daggers at old Augustus.

"Don't go giving the boy wrong ideas," Bryna scolds her husband. She is, for a change, in complete agreement with her daughter-in-law.

"Boy? Boy?" says Augustus. "Maximilian's not a boy, he's a *man!*"

"I'll drink to that," says Henry Glick, sliding his glass toward his father. A bit shakily, Augustus fills his son's glass again and proceeds to fill the glasses of the other men, only one of whom — Rabbi Teitelman — resists gently, though in vain. The women once again cover their glasses self-righteously, but are unable to hide their amusement at the creeping unsteadiness of Augustus — the self-appointed bartender — and his willing patrons. Rabbi Teitelman, by now slurring his consonants, suggests to his Lubavitch colleagues that a little music might be in order.

"Fine with me," says Reuben Calish agreeably. "My accordion's in the van. The only question is: can I make it to the van and back?" He jiggles his brandy glass which has been filled and emptied three or four times; he's not sure how often, having lost count.

"I'll get my clarinet," says Corey Silverstone, "but somebody else may have to blow it."

Manny Kirsch, the drummer, declines to fetch his set of drums. "I'll just use the tabletop. It'll save everybody's ears, including mine."

All move to the Glick livingroom — old Augustus carrying the remains of the second bottle of brandy in one hand and a newly opened bottle in the other. Within minutes the house shudders, its walls and ceilings under attack from Calish's accordion, Silverstone's clarinet, and Kirsch's snare drum which, he has decided after all, works better than a tabletop.

At the center of the livingroom stands Horrible Herman Hitzik, miles removed now from car-sickness; indeed the brandy has removed him from most of his earthly cares. He is poised for dancing, waiting only for the tempo of the music to match the slow undulation of his shoulders. He has taken the liberty of shedding his black coat. Streaks of gray run down the front and back of his white shirt where he perspires. Horrible Herman Hitzik, unlike his partners, is of slight build, and as he positions himself to dance, pointing the toe of his small right foot outward and slightly to the side and tapping it to the beat of the music, there is something delicate, almost feminine, in his posture. Now he performs the same step with his left foot, deftly, gracefully, like a ballerina. The shoulders continue to roll, the head thrown back proudly. And suddenly, from this tiny lean man there comes a sound like an air-raid siren; it floats up and out, it seems to carry with it a thousand years of wild joy, indescribable sorrow, sung at a pitch that would split a mountain. His audience, mesmerized, begins to clap in time, slowly, deliberately.

Maximilian recognizes the language of the lyric — Hebrew — but cannot follow the words. "What's he singing?" he asks Rabbi Teitelman.

Without losing the beat, Teitelman, still clapping, answers — "It's an old Hasidic song" — he leans close to Max. "It's about life's uncertainties and how they're all part of God's will. It praises God for constantly testing his people." Max notes that, while there is little hesitation in the rabbi's reply, his speech has thickened, his eyelid droops a little, his red hair is matted with sweat around his forehead. The rabbi's breath, only inches away, reminds Maximilian of Derek Blackthorn's; the odor of alcohol seems even to exude from his pores.

The pace of the music accelerates steadily until it borders on the furious, yet the musicians, thorough professionals, have no difficulty maintaining it. Accordion and clarinet interlace their melodic parts in an intricate pattern. Manny Kirsch's sticks beat against the skin of his snare drum with the swiftness of hummingbird wings. Herman Hitzik's dancing — at first almost dainty — is now peasanty and foot-stomping, executed with such zest and abandon that the floor of the Glick house — built to last a century — seems on the verge of collapse.

Suddenly Teitelman lets out a "Whoop!" and is on his feet. The dance at the center of the floor has become a duet. Laughing, whooping like farmhands at a hoedown, the two whirl, spin, kick, their white socks and black shoes flashing high into the air.

A bit anxiously, Sarah Glick eyes the fireplace mantle where a pair of antique Chinese vases, acquired only recently, after hard bargaining, from Doc Ingoldsby, have begun a sympathetic rattle. Next to them, a delicate perpetual clock vibrates perilously close to the end of its time and its mahogany perch. But just as she makes a discreet move to protect her treasures, and just as startlingly as they began, the music and dancing cease. Hitzik and Teitelman, flushed from their efforts, give a final yelp, then reel away from each other. Hitzik, the professional, feigns dizziness, but Teitelman is genuinely dazed. With some difficulty he picks out his chair and flops himself into it, flattening the down cushions into pancakes. (Sarah Glick makes a mental note to fluff the cushions first chance she gets.)

Now Augustus Glick has the center of the floor, brandy bottle in hand, and Henry has produced fresh glasses.

Sarah shoots a meaningful glance at her husband. "These gentlemen have a long drive ahead of them tomorrow, Henry —"

"Nonsense!" says Henry. "Tomorrow's tomorrow. Tonight we drink!"

The men cheer, all except Teitelman who is still trying to catch his breath.

"You're outa shape, Rabbi, if you'll pardon my saying so," says Henry Glick. He hands Teitelman a small glass of brandy. "Here . . . just what the doctor ordered."

In a stupor, the young rabbi grips the glass and downs the brandy heroically. He slumps back in his chair, the whites of his eyes as red as his beard.

Augustus Glick raises his own brandy glass. "A toast everyone!" he shouts. "I want to propose a toast —"

"No . . . wait," Teitelman interrupts thickly. "It's my turn . . . to pre-pose a toasht. Thass a rabbi's per . . . a rabbi's p'rogatiff."

The young man struggles to his feet, extending his glass for another refill. Reuben Calish says: "Three cheers for Teitelman!" as Augustus Glick pours obligingly. "You'll drown the poor man," says Bryna, but the old man isn't paying attention to her. "The floor's yours," he says to the rabbi, adding only half in jest: "Now mind what you say, young fella. We don't want a repeat of the other night."

"Not to worry," says the rabbi. "I have complete control of all my f-faculties." Teitelman stops here, his lips pressed together, his eyes closed. All systems within are temporarily shut down, perhaps for emergency repair, perhaps to allow energy to build so he can plunge into his next thoughts. Abruptly his eyes open wide; they focus on some object at the tip of his nose, while his glass, once again empty, is held high. "A toast!" says the rabbi. "A toast to music . . . that soothes the savage breast . . . or is it beast? . . . I always forget which. To music . . . to the great D-Dionysus —"

Maximilian whispers to Henry Glick: "Who's Dionysus?"

Plucking a fact from his unused college philosophy, Henry replies: "The Greek god of Wine and Music."

To Max it seems strange that a rabbi should be toasting a Greek god of anything, let alone wine and music. But no one else in the room seems perturbed. It is a night, Maximilian concludes, for the absurd. He has never before experienced anything quite like it. At most adult gatherings, the women take over the livingroom where the discussion runs to recipes — for baking, for raising children, for raising funds for the local synagogue or Israel. And the men segregate themselves in the diningroom where they deal with questions of national politics, international trade, and other matters about which they can do nothing. Before midnight somebody always points out that it's late, that tomorrow's another day; then, quietly, decently, two-by-two, as if heading for Noah's Ark, the company departs and drives off in solid, four-door sedans.

In the Glick livingroom everyone's attention is on Rabbi Teitelman. The young man's face has never looked whiter, his eyes never redder. "Where was I?" asks the rabbi, vaguely aware that he is in the midst of making a speech.

"Dionysus," Reuben Calish reminds him. "The Greek god."

Henry Glick looks over at Maximilian and smiles with satisfaction, underlining for his son's benefit the obvious value of a higher education.

"Speaking of which," the Lubavitcher rabbi says, working hard to keep his words from running into each other, "we have . . . tonight . . . right here . . . on our very own stage —"

Oh no! Oh no! says Maximilian to himself.

"Maximilian Glick. . . ." Pointing over to the boy, like a master of ceremonies, the rabbi calls out: "Steelton's own god of music!"

Oh no! Maximilian repeats to himself.

Reuben Calish grins at Max with delight. "You're a musician too?"

But before the boy can answer, the rabbi is standing behind him, prodding gently. "C'mon Max, to the piano, boy."

Max blushes and hangs back. "I better not . . . not tonight — "

"Just one eentsy-teentsy n-number," Teitelman insists.

"I'm out of practice —"

"Nonsense, dear," says Bryna Glick. "You're *never* out of practice."

"Mother," says Sarah Glick, coming to her son's aid, "he's a bit shy."

"Besides," Max adds, "I wouldn't know what to play. I mean, I don't know any Jewish pieces."

"It doesn't have to be a Jewish piece," Reuben Calish coaxes. "Play anything."

"Play Mozart's 'Turkish Rondo,' or that other piece . . . by Beethoven . . . you know the one I mean Maxie —" Bryna hums the first bar of "Für Elise." "They're both Jewish." To Bryna Glick, anything written in a minor key is Jewish, even if the composer is from Borneo.

Pushed firmly toward the Bechstein by Teitelman and urged on by the others (except Sarah Glick, who senses his shyness under these conditions), Maximilian seats himself at the keyboard and plays — beautifully — a short but melodic piece. To discourage encores, he rises quickly from the bench.

"Encore! Encore!" call the visitors from Detroit, applauding.

"Didn't I tell you the k-kid's great!" says Teitelman, the proud impresario, to his fellow Lubavitchers.

Reuben Calish asks Max: "What was that? I've heard it before, but I can't remember the name."

"It was one of the 'Songs Without Words,' by Felix Mendelssohn."

"You see," says Bryna Glick to Max, "you *do* know some Jewish pieces. Felix Mendelssohn was a Jew."

Augustus Glick is unimpressed. "Not much of a Jew, if you ask me. Didn't his family convert to Christianity? I think Mendelssohn was raised as a Christian, as a matter of fact."

"Maybe so," Bryna Glick allows, "but it didn't stop him from being a great composer. Whose 'Wedding March' do you think they played when you and I got married? And when Henry and Sarah got married? I didn't hear you objecting at the time, Augustus."

Grumpily, Augustus Glick says: "You know how I feel about Jews who get mixed up with Christianity, Bryna."

"That's not the point. The man is one thing, his music is another."

"Not in my books," says Augustus flatly. "You don't separate the man from his work, as far as I'm concerned." He turns to Reuben Calish. "In this world you're either a Jew or you're not a Jew, and there's nothing in between, isn't that right?"

"That's certainly *our* position on the question," says Reuben Calish. "Being Jewish is not a hobby ... not just something you take up and put down, like a book of short stories. It's a round-the-clock kind of thing. I'm sure your own rabbi agrees with me a hundred percent." He looks over at Kalman Teitelman for expected support.

Teitelman's ears are stuffed with cotton-batting, his tongue anaesthetized inside his mouth. He can feel cold beads of perspiration trickling from his hairline down his forehead and temples. He knows the debate has something to do with Jewishness and that somebody — he's not sure who — has asked him if something is one hundred percent certain. In some buried reservoir that has no connection with his vocal chords, he locates a loose string of words and hears himself reply to Calish: "Pard'n me for muddying the w-waters, but nothing is a h-hun'rd p'rcent certain. What I mean is ... the only thing that's a hun'red percent certain is that *nothing* is a hun'red percent certain." Rather pleased with the way he has put this, the rabbi smiles to himself.

Augustus Glick is bristling. Once again this Lubavitcher is proving unreliable. "Now surely, Rabbi," he says, "you're not going to stand there and tell us you're in favor of compromising our religious beliefs, our traditions? *You* ... of all people ... a Lubavitcher?"

Calish, though taken aback at Teitelman's Theory of Uncertainty, moves to his colleague's defence. "I'm sure what the rabbi meant was that —"

Teitelman interrupts: "I can speak for myself, thank you," he says politely to Calish. Though he stands unsteadily, his face has a determined look. "It's the rabbi's per ... p'rogative to speak for himself, right? ..." Hearing no contrary opinion, Teitelman goes on, looking straight at Augustus Glick: "My dear sir: is A. Glick & Son's furniture emporium open ... or closed ... on the Jewish Sabbath ... Saturday?"

"Well now, it's open but —"

"And do you or do you not frequent Hong Ling's China Palace?"

The old man speaks quickly. "I don't touch a thing that's got pork in it. Not a mouthful!"

"And when was the last time you took the time to put on your tefillin and say the morning prayers before you went to work?"

"I can't remember the exact date, of course, but —"

"Ah," says Teitelman, "the answer should have been *this morning* ... if you were a *hundred* p-percent Jew."

Though separated by a large coffee table, old Augustus Glick and the young rabbi now seem to stand toe-to-toe, with the older man clearly losing ground. "But, but, you're overlooking certain realities of life in Steelton," Augustus Glick stammers.

Teitelman, however, is not inclined to be merciful. "Even *you*, my friend, are a compromiser, are you not?"

"But —"

"And yet you would presume to judge others? To say:

'This man is an okay Jew but that man isn't an okay Jew so let's throw him and all his work out the window' ... that's what you would presume t-to do?"

Augustus Glick glares at the rabbi. The rabbi seems to be propped up by nothing more than sheer nerve. He is too bleary-eyed to glare back. Silently, like seconds at a duel, Henry Glick has risen to stand behind his father, his calming hand on the old man's shoulder, and Reuben Calish has stationed himself behind Rabbi Teitelman. "Maybe you should sit for a minute, you'll feel better, Rabbi," Calish whispers.

Brusquely the rabbi waves off his advisor. "I'm fine ... never felt better...."

Sarah Glick is solicitous. "Can I get you some black coffee?" she suggests to the rabbi. But this too is rejected. Teitelman's gaze — as much of it as can work its way past his drooping eyelids — fixes on his adversary. "Anybody, my dear sir," he says to Augustus Glick, "*any*body can fall from grace. There's no such thing as a perfect Jew ... and you, sir, are the perfect example of that perfect fact!"

Though the senior Glick has also had too much to drink, his jaw — jowls and all — juts out bellicosely, and he clenches his knobby old fists.

Maximilian stares at both men with fascination. In his wildest imagination he cannot see either striking a blow at the other. But then ... the night has already proven bizarre. Who knows where the craziness will stop?

Henry Glick says soothingly to his father: "Dad, why don't we all sit down? Sarah'll make some fresh coffee —"

Sarah Glick rises from her chair. "Good idea," she says.

"No, wait. I don't need coffee." Angrily Augustus points to Rabbi Teitelman: "This man ... this man has slandered my family's name and reputation ... a reputation that has gone without stain for generations ... and that'll go on without stain for generations to come!"

"You have no power to speak for the generations to come, sir," Teitelman responds, punctuating his response with a jolting hiccup.

"Is that so? Are you telling *me* I don't know my own children ... my own grandson —" The old man becomes watery-eyed. "My own dear grandson ... flesh of my flesh, blood of my blood —"

Sarah Glick is equally solicitous to her father-in-law. "Dad, please, take it easy. Let me get you a cup of coffee."

"I said I don't need coffee —"

"Gus!" It is Bryna Glick now, employing her husband's nickname, usually a sign that he is being intemperate, immodest, impatient, or a plain nuisance. "Gus!", snapped imperiously, usually achieves an immediate and beneficial result, but this time falls on deaf ears. Still clench-fisted, eyeing Kalman Teitelman like a cautious prizefighter, old Augustus Glick says through gritted teeth: "Rabbi Kaminsky, may he rest in peace, wouldn't have made such a statement ... not in a million years."

"Gentlemen, gentlemen!" Reuben Calish calls out, trying to play the role of peacemaker. He positions himself between the old man and the young rabbi, a benign smile showing through his thick beard and mustache. He holds up his hands, a referee calling an end to a match. "Come now, are we not all Jews?"

The old man jerks his thumb at the Lubavitcher rabbi. "Apparently not, according to *your* sort."

Calish allows this slur to roll past him. Without losing his smile, he looks first to the rabbi, then to the senior Glick. "Let us have peace, gentlemen. After all, God willing, you two will dwell side by side in the House of the Lord for many years to come."

"Maybe God's willing," says Augustus Glick, still hot, "but *I'm* not. Not so long as this man insists on throwing up our imperfections into our faces all the time."

Teitelman, still groping his way through an alcoholic fog, retorts: "I haven't thrown up anything —"

"You do it all the time —"

"I do *not* —"

Calish, the peacemaker, smiling like a saint, holds up his

hands once more. "All right boys," he says, as if talking to errant youngsters, "now that we've got that off our chests, why don't we all sit down . . . and calm down . . . nicely. Okay?" He turns to Sarah Glick. "At the risk of being a pushy guest, that coffee idea sounds awfully good to me. Could we trouble you?"

"Of course," says Sarah Glick, making for the kitchen.

Augustus Glick takes a seat on one side of the large coffee table; Rabbi Teitelman takes a seat on the other. "There," says Calish, "that's more like it." Again the saintly smile, the hushed tone of voice.

There is total silence. No one stirs. The storm seems to be over.

Suddenly, Augustus Glick leans forward in his chair pugnaciously. "You wanna run an old timer like me into the ground, maybe that's your privilege. Then again, maybe it's not. But there's one thing for sure . . . I will not stand for one bad word about young Maximilian here, and I don't care if you're the Chief Rabbi of Jerusalem!" The old man's voice chokes.

Again Reuben Calish motions for a truce, but before he can utter a syllable the rabbi gets to his feet, holding one arm of his chair for support. "I never said a bad word about Maximil . . . Max. Me and him . . . I mean he and I . . . are friends. Izzn' that so, Max?"

Maximilian nods, figuring a nod is a bit more neutral than an outright "Yes."

"An' I'll tell you s-something else, my dear sir," Rabbi Teitelman says, still gripping the arm of his chair for support. "Someday . . . someday when Maxie here finally escapes from this . . . this c-cocoon an' heads for New York City with Celia . . . What's-her-name . . . we'll just see who does all the bad-mouthing around here."

Henry Glick's brow furrows slightly. "Celia who? What're you talking about, Rabbi?"

"You know, Celia What's-her-name . . . Brzjinski. Of the famous team of Brzjinski and Glick —" He leans toward

Maximilian. "Or is it Glick and Brzjinski, Max?"

Maximilian feels himself turn into stone. This *has* to be a bad dream, he tells himself; there is no other explanation.

All eyes on Max, his father quietly asks: "Max, what's this business about Glick and Brzjinski? I don't understand."

The boy is speechless.

"Maxie, what's this all about? I want to know."

Maximilian shakes his head. "Nothing."

"Then why do you look so upset?"

"Who's upset?"

"You are, obviously."

Max protests half-heartedly: "I'm not upset ... honest."

Bryna Glick suddenly springs to life. "Brzjinski ... isn't that the name of the girl who almost tied with you at the music festival? Yes, of course, I remember now." Maximilian's grandmother throws back her head and laughs. "Well, well, Maxie, don't tell me you and your arch rival are having a love affair!" She laughs again.

"Max," Henry Glick says sternly, "I demand to know what's going on here —"

Bryna Glick interrupts. "Really, Henry, there are times when you and your father haven't the sense of humor of a turtle. Haven't you ever heard of puppy love?"

"Puppy love doesn't include running off to New York City —"

Max feels himself turning into fire.

One of the visiting Lubavitchers, Herman Hitzik, the singer, says lightheartedly: "Well, if it's puppy love, at least it's between Jewish puppies." The other visitors chuckle.

"That's just the point," says Henry Glick. "The Brzjinskis are not a Jewish family."

The visiting Lubavitchers are suddenly sober. "Ah, I see," says Hitzik, full of sympathy for the anxious parent. To the boy he says: "So, Maxie, you really planning to go to New York City? There's a wonderful Lubavitch community there. It's in a section of Brooklyn called Williamsburg. I could give you some names to look up in Williamsburg. My cousin Shloime is a diamond-cutter there, and he's got a daughter about your age." Herman Hitzik smacks his lips. "She's a living doll, Maxie! Plays the flute. Hey, maybe you could be her accompanist!"

Henry Glick scarcely hears any of this. His concerns are largely local. "Who are these Brzjinskis?" he asks Augustus.

"He's a builder. That's all I know about him. She's been in the store coupla times."

"Who? The girl?"

"No, the mother. Lots of money, but no taste."

Henry returns to Maximilian. "What's this about New York?"

"It's only a joke."

"A joke?" Henry Glick is skeptical. "Then how come *we* haven't been in on it? Or is it something you share only with the rabbi?"

"I didn't really mean it's a joke ... what I mean is —"

Maximilian's eyes brand Kalman Teitelman's whitish face. It is at this point that the Great Hand that parted the Red Sea goes to work again, this time to lift the fog just enough to enable the young rabbi to perceive the wreckage his unthinking tongue has caused. "Oh my God!" he whispers hoarsely. He blinks hard at Maximilian. "I'm sorry ... Max, old friend, I'm sorry —"

In a flat quiet voice, Max stops him: "I'm not your friend."

Henry Glick, struggling to be civil, says: "Rabbi, I must insist ... if you know something about Max that we ought to know —"

The rabbi only ignores this interrogation. Over and over again he repeats: "I'm sorry, Max ... sorry...."

Sarah Glick, re-entering the room with cups and saucers, senses immediately that while she has been brewing coffee the occupants — or some of them — have been brewing a fresh storm in the livingroom. "What's wrong?" she asks Bryna Glick.

"Our husbands are having a conniption over a silly little matter."

"It is *not* silly," says Augustus Glick. "Why don't you butt out, Bryna."

"I beg your pardon!" Bryna Glick yells at her husband.

"Beg anything you like," he yells back, "just so long as you butt out."

"Dad," Henry Glick pleads, "take it easy —"

"You're a fine one to be telling *me* to take it easy," Augustus tells his son. "You started it all."

"Who started *what*?" Sarah Glick asks.

"Our son," says Henry to Sarah, "has some cockeyed plan about running off to New York City with this girl . . . this Celia Whatever-her-name-is."

"New York City?" Sarah, half-frowning, half-smiling, puts down the tray, and looks squarely at the boy. "Maxie, what on earth? —"

"Oh let the poor kid alone," Bryna says testily.

"Mother," says Sarah, "leave this to me . . . *please*."

Henry, also testy, says: "Sarah, there's no need to talk to my mother that way —"

Weakly, Rabbi Teitelman keeps interjecting "It's my fault . . . *I* started it all —" But no one seems to be listening to the Lubavitcher now. Without knowing precisely what they are arguing about, suspecting that something vaguely sinister is afoot between Maximilian — the apple of their eye — and this outcast girl sent by the devil to blight that apple, the Glick family fire and cross-fire at each other from their individual battle stations in the livingroom. In the hail of verbal bullets no one notices or cares that Rabbi Teitelman has sunk back into his chair. A watery film obscures his eyes. His pale hands hang limply between his knees. The toes of his black shoes, pointing inward, touch tragically.

Nor do the Glicks notice that Maximilian is quietly, stealthily, making his way out of the livingroom. Kalman Teitelman notices. He calls out "Max . . . wait —"

But the boy's face, as he passes from Teitelman's view through the archway, makes it clear that all paths of communication are sealed off. Perhaps forever.

Part Three

14

As far as Maximilian Glick was concerned, the sky had fallen upon his private hopes and ambitions. And who had caused the sky to fall? In the courtroom of his mind he placed Kalman Teitelman on trial. The charge: Treason. The verdict: Guilty!

And what ought the penalty to be? Something suitably biblical, thought Maximilian. Banishment outside the gates of Steelton. An eye for an eye. Stoning. All three, maybe. Or again, something even more terrible, something inspired by the Industrial Age, involving complicated machinery, electricity, and bubbling vats of chemicals, straight out of science fiction.

These thoughts cast long shadows across the boy's waking hours. Nor were his sleeping hours any better. Revenge is a restless bedmate.

To make matters worse, there had been a confrontation with his father and mother later that night, after their Detroit guests — murmuring awkward thanks and apologies — bundled themselves and the rabbi into the Mitzva-mobile and fled the disaster site. Max's parents made their position clear to him: music was one of life's pleasanter decorations, a nice finishing touch, something to be indulged in when the real cares and concerns of the day were over. Make no mistake about it, they said; the real world was the world of facts and figures, diseases and cures, money in the bank for rainy days and old age. Go off to New York City to study music? Never! And compound the disgrace by getting mixed up with — and,

Heaven forbid, marrying — a Gentile girl? Out of the question!

Especially humiliating to Maximilian were the reactions of his grandparents. Bryna Glick, by pooh-poohing the whole thing as a simple case of puppy love (with overtones of international travel), served only to irritate both her son, who thought she grossly underestimated the gravity of the matter, and her grandson, to whom the term "puppy love" was nothing short of an insult. Whether she meant to or not, she had taken his relationship with Celia Brzjinski and pinned diapers on it. As for Grandfather Glick, having rattled his dull sabre at the outset, he now elected to retire to the hills from which, like a tired old general, he could observe at a safe distance the tribulations in the valley below.

Maximilian's gloominess did not escape the attentive eyes and ears of Derek Blackthorn. Midway through a Chopin waltz, Blackthorn touched his pupil's arm.

Max stopped playing. "Yes, Mr. Blackthorn?"

"Max," said Blackthorn, "it's a waltz, my boy, a waltz. Not dance music for King Kong."

Ordinarily, Maximilian would have accepted such well-meant criticism with a smile and begun again. This time, however, he hung his head over the keyboard and rested his fingertips lifelessly at the edge of the keys.

"What's the trouble, Mr. Glick? Not your week for waltzes?" joked Blackthorn.

"It's not my week for anything," Maximilian muttered.

Blackthorn looked at him closely. "Well, Max, I'm only a lowly piano teacher, not a psychiatrist, but would you like to tell me about it?"

While Maximilian finally related the story of the fateful supper, Blackthorn listened patiently, without once interrupting the boy's tale. When Max had finished, the piano teacher nodded his head thoughtfully. "Ahah ... hm...." He paced back and forth several times, his bony fingers interlocked behind his back, creasing the already rumpled corduroy jacket. His ever-present cigarette dangled from his lower lip, the smoke drifting upward into his eyes, forcing him to squint. Looking pensive, he puffed on. Finally, he stopped pacing and took a chair next to the piano. "How old are you, Max?"

"Thirteen . . . in September."

"Yes, of course. In September."

"Why?"

Blackthorn examined his pupil through the cloud of smoke. A long ash clung supernaturally to the end of his cigarette; then, on the next puff, it released its hold and joined some others, along with two or three food stains, on his lapels. "It strikes me, Maximilian," he said slowly, without removing the butt from between his teeth, "that the world has expected a great deal from you."

"My name's mostly to blame for that, according to my grandmother."

"It also strikes me. . . ." At this point Blackthorn removed the cigarette and ground its remains into an empty teacup. "It also strikes me that you . . . as a result . . . expect a great deal from the world."

"I don't know what you mean," Maximilian said.

"Well, take this rabbi for instance . . . what's his name, Teitelman? Do you think he intended to do you harm?"

"I don't know."

"Well, was there even a hint of malice in what he did or said?"

Maximilian shook his head. "How should I know? He'd had too much to drink. He was disgusting."

"Yes, I know, Max. That's a condition with which I've had some familiarity in my lifetime."

"I know," said Max. He hadn't intended to admit that he knew about Blackthorn's drinking; it had simply slipped out. "I'm sorry . . . what I meant was — "

"You needn't be embarrassed," said Blackthorn. "My wife and I have learned one thing since settling in Steelton: everybody knows everything. It's one of the more charming aspects of smalltown life. I'm sure your rather peculiar friend in the black hat and red beard has learned the same lesson by this time."

"I don't see what all this has to do with me," Max said. "All I care about is that he got drunk and shot his mouth off. I kept *my* end of the bargain — "

"What bargain, Max?"

"I've never told a soul about his deepest secret . . . that he wants to be a comedian, and still spends a lot of his time dreaming up jokes. And I never will."

"But you've just told *me!*" said Blackthorn. He peered intently into his pupil's face. "Don't you see, Max, how easy . . . how terribly easy it is for people to be less than perfect?"

"But telling you now . . . it's not the same — "

"Oh yes it is, Max; yes it is! If you'd kept the rabbi's secret perfectly, you wouldn't have breathed so much as a word of it . . . not even a syllable . . . not to me, not to anybody. What I'm getting at, Max, is that life is really a sloppy business. It's full of missed trains, unmade beds, friendships that are put together like puzzles and come apart the same way. You may make a lot of things in this life, my friend: money, contacts . . . but nothing is more important than making allowances."

Blackthorn paused to light up another cigarette, inhaling deeply, as if it were his first of the day. "You want to know what a fellow like me is doing in a town like Steelton?" he then asked, in an almost off-hand manner. "I'm sure you've heard a hundred and one stories on the subject . . . all of them pure speculation, I hasten to add. Most of 'em come back to me in one form or another. Some old crust by the name of Moskover has been going around town lately telling people Shizuko and I are a team of spies. Last year's rumor was that I'd killed a man in a duel in Mexico and Interpol was looking for me. The year before that, I was a deserter from the French Foreign Legion. Shizuko is supposed to be a fugitive from justice too. Landed on the coast of California from a Japanese submarine a few days before Pearl Harbor for the purpose of reporting movements of U.S. warships out of San Diego. A neat trick, considering Shiz was six years old at the time. I'm sure you've heard most of this nonsense before, Max."

Maximilian hesitated. "Well. . . ."

"You can be frank, Max. We're talking man to man."

"I didn't know Mrs. Blackthorn was only six at the time."

Blackthorn laughed. "She'll be furious with me. She guards her age like the Royal Mint. Anyway, all that's beside the point — " He paused to butt the latest cigarette in the same empty teacup, withdrew another from the package beside the keyboard, and held it, unlit, between his long fingers. It seemed to Max that, whatever one heard about the evils of cigarettes, to Derek Blackthorn they were a life-support system, even unlit.

Legs extended before him, long and parallel, like a pair of skis, Blackthorn slouched back in his armchair. He went on: "Back in 1946, I was fresh out of the Royal Air Force. I'd been a fighter pilot for three-and-a-half years, seen action over Europe, North Africa, been shot up, shot sideways, shot down ... as you know. Did more living in those three-and-a-half years than most people do in a lifetime. I'd put in a couple of years at the Royal College of Music before I went into the service, and managed to keep up with my studies to some extent during off-hours in the air force ... that is, when I wasn't busy pounding out 'Roll Out the Barrel' on the mess-hall piano for a bunch of drunken pals. Anyway, I did some serious composing, two or three orchestral things ... including a suite for strings I thought was quite good. The suite was really pretty sketchy, but I intended to have a steady go at it now that the war was over. I showed the sketches to my Uncle Basil ... *Sir* Basil Blackthorn. He was the music director of the London Philharmonic in those days. A very Edwardian character ... always wore a cutaway coat and striped pants, even when he went to the seaside in summer. All the great English composers at one time or another were obliged to embrace dear Uncle Basil's rather ample posterior in order to get their works played by the Philharmonic. That was a fact of musical life in England. But I — being the man's nephew, and being a bit of a war hero, at least in my own eyes — made the mistake of assuming that he would grasp immediately the enormity of my genius and schedule at least one of

my works for the first available concert. This is probably
boring you stiff, Glick — "

"No no, honest!" Maximilian said, pleased that only he, in
all of Steelton, was privileged to hear the inside story.

"Well, much to my chagrin, dear Uncle Basil gave my work
no more than a cursory look. I'm sure he spent more time
searching through the *London Times* that day to see if his
name was in print. 'Derek my boy,' he said, 'war has a brutal-
izing effect on composers, and I'm afraid your stuff is proof
of that sad truth.' He was referring to the fact that I'd used
some rather harsh discords here and there ... nothing more
shocking than, say, Stravinsky or Prokofiev had used, though
in all honesty it wasn't exactly the sort of tune you left the
concert hall whistling. Anyway, Max, by the time he instructed
his butler to show me to the door, I'd called him a doddering
old fool and he'd called me an insolent young fool, and that
was the end of nepotism in the Blackthorn dynasty."

"Nepitism? — "

"Ne-*po*-tism. Look it up when you get home, Max. To continue: the first thing I did, after being ushered out of Uncle
Basil's flat, was to head straight for the nearest pub — "

"Pub? — "

"Tavern. Booze-ateria. Drinkatorium."

"Right."

"And at the pub I proceeded to get drunk, so drunk in fact
that the proprietor showed me to *his* door where a kindly
policeman, perceiving by the button in my lapel that I was a
war veteran, hailed a cab to take me home, instead of hauling
me in for being disorderly in a public place. Inside the cab
things only got worse. I don't know what it was ... I didn't
like the color of the cabbie's shirt, I think ... and half-way
home he pulled over to the curb and showed me *his* door. I
got out ... or rather fell out, muttering unprintable epithets
about the working classes of England ... at which point another constable, this time less charitable, hailed a patrol car,
and off I went to an Elizabethan dungeon for vagrants ... a
place that made Devil's Island look like the Ritz. It wasn't

until the middle of that night, when I began to sober up, that I realized that somewhere along my descent into Hell I'd lost my manuscripts. In the morning, the magistrate, who also perceived the button in my lapel, let me off with a lecture about the proper way to rehabilitate oneself after an armistice. I don't think I heard a word of it. I could only think that my precious manuscripts were lost, and I had no copies. All that day I retraced my steps ... which was no easy task considering my steps had been, shall we say, multi-directional; also I'd been thrown out of a flat, a pub, and a cab, and it was a bit difficult to go back to my hosts for assistance under the circumstances."

"Did you ever find the manuscripts?"

"Never. Well, I stewed for several days, and decided that all this havoc was the fault of Uncle Basil. And I vowed to create double-havoc. I'd show *him* what it meant to be brutalized by *peace*, let alone by war. You sure I'm not boring you, Glick? Perhaps you've a date with the fair Miss Brzjinski — "

"I'm meeting Celia later for a Coke. It's okay, though...."

"Several days went by; then I hit on a plan. I got hold of a chest of carpenter's tools, a beat-up tweed cap, a pair of workman's boots. Posing as a maintenance man, I got past the night watchman of the concert hall where Uncle Basil was to conduct the Philharmonic next evening. You must understand that, being an Edwardian, my uncle over-ate much of the time. Sir Basil Blackthorn carried a lot of weight in English musical circles, literally as well as figuratively. Which was precisely what I was counting on. With my carpenter's tools I lifted the carpet that was tacked to the conductor's podium. Then, with such skill that even *I* was amazed, I took a fine saw and cut the strips of flooring on the podium ... not all the way through, mind you, but just sufficiently so that, under a certain degree of strain, they would give way. I knew that the opening number on his program would be Wagner's overture to *Die Meistersinger* which begins with some good loud chords and calls for a succession of heavy downbeats on the part of the conductor. Then I tacked the carpet back into place like a real professional, bid the night watchman goodnight, and vanished into the London fog. My God, I *do* apologize, Max; I'm sure your arteries must be hardening out of sheer boredom — "

"God no!"

Shrewdly, Blackthorn pretended to be skeptical. "You sure?"

"Absolutely!"

"Very well then. Next evening there I was, way up in the upper tier of the concert hall . . . in the cheap seats . . . waiting, praying, mentally rechecking my calculations. Mass–times–velocity equals the Great Downward Plunge. And then, at last, the house lights dimmed. And out from the wings strode Sir Humphrey Bassett, substituting for Uncle Basil who'd taken ill at the last minute . . . probably from over-eating. Sir Humphrey Bassett had been my composition professor at the Royal College before the war. Great friend of contemporary music. I worshipped the man. Good God, what was I to do? As he mounted the podium, I stood up. My throat went dry. I half-shouted: 'Wait! There's been a mistake!' Two ushers nearby motioned fiercely to me to sit down and shut up. Before I could utter another sound, Sir Humphrey — who was also a very large man — brought his baton down firmly and the overture to *Die Meistersinger* began . . . dum, dum, de-dum. And then, at the end of the fourth bar, precisely as I'd planned it, there was the conductor, suddenly up to his knees in lumber . . . awash in a sea of English oak and English carpet . . . the fruit of England's forests and looms.

"Well, my usher friends — they must have got their training at Scotland Yard — immediately put two and two together. Within the hour I found myself in yet another Elizabethan dungeon, this time for felons who tamper with podiums. At my trial I pleaded guilty. There was no point in doing otherwise; the night watchman's identification was dead-on. The press got hold of the story and had great fun with it, of course. 'Famed Conductor's Nephew Slices Up Podium' . . . etcetera etcetera. Again because of my veteran's status, I got off with a suspended sentence. But as far as my family was concerned, there were no subtleties, no sensitivities, no honest human emotions involved in the affair. I'd committed a crime. What's more, I'd committed it stupidly. Never mind why. Uncle Basil sent a note to my folks saying I was never to defile his doorstep again . . . that he'd see to it I never got a job in music in Britain, except polishing somebody's tuba. My father was a tax accountant. *He* classified me as a total write-off.

"Anyway, there was therefore only one course open to me: exile. So off I went to New Zealand, an Englishman's Siberia. Served a life sentence for the next five years as a choir master in a small Anglican church. Took off for Australia. Another life sentence . . . this time three years as a music teacher at a private school for girls. At the end of those eight years, I wrote home to England proposing to return. My father sent back my letter unopened. 'Return To Sender' . . . Appeal denied! The next decade of my life has no fixed place of abode. I worked, wandered, squandered, bummed, drank, read with no sorrow at all that my distinguished uncle had passed on to that Great Restaurant in the Sky, learned with much sorrow that Sir Humphrey Bassett had died — "

Derek Blackthorn paused. In the dark circles around his deep brown eyes Maximilian had always noted a touch of sadness, but at the mention of Sir Humphrey Bassett's demise, those eyes took on a faraway look, as though recalling the sight of something, or someone, lost forever. Max expected his teacher to light the waiting cigarette at this point, but it remained unlit, perhaps out of respect for the late Sir Humphrey.

After a moment or two, Blackthorn resumed: "To this day I'm not sure exactly how I landed on the west coast of Canada. I recall distinctly that I called home from Vancouver. I figured with Uncle Basil out of the picture, maybe the expatriate could return at last to his native land. My older sister answered the telephone. I could almost hear her rubbing her spinster's hands with glee as she announced that my parents, first my mother, then my father, had passed away a year or so earlier, leaving everything to her. I reacted to this news by drinking everything the City of Vancouver had to offer . . . within the space of twenty-four hours. I think I passed out on the sidewalk outside the local Sally Ann — "

"Sally Ann? — "

"Salvation Army to you, Max. Ended up in hospital where they dried me out like a biscuit. One day they sent in a social worker to see if they could raise my attention span back to an adult level. The social worker was a young Japanese woman, and . . . well, it turned out we had something in common: I wanted to get out of hospital; she wanted to get out of social work. We made the break together. With scarcely a cent to our names, we headed east, hoping to make it to Spain where she would resume her first love . . . ceramics. I would go back to my suite for strings, doing the best I could to reconstruct it from memory."

"Did you make it to Spain?"

"Our money ran out. So did our luck. We made it to beautiful Steelton-by-the-Sea. No farther."

"Do you think you will ever get to Spain?" Max asked.

Again, Blackthorn's eyes took on their sad faraway look. Then, in a sudden change of mood, he said: "See here, Glick, where do you get off asking personal questions of that sort?"

Confused and taken aback by this, Max said: "I don't get it. You were just telling me your life story — "

"I was doing nothing of the sort," said Blackthorn coolly. "The entire tale is a tissue of lies."

"Then why? — "

Blackthorn rose from his armchair, transforming himself from a semi-horizontal slouching figure to a figure that towered over his young pupil seated on the piano bench.

"I lied to you a moment ago, Max. The story I told you was indeed true."

"True?"

"True. Every word of it. But then again, it's false . . . flimsy as gossamer . . . a network of vapor trails. No sane person would ever tell such a story. No sane person would ever *believe* it. Don't you agree?"

"I . . . I uh. . . ." Maximilian was incapable of responding. He felt as if he'd just been spun round and round, deliberately made dizzy. He began to feel resentful. Why had Blackthorn toyed with him, made him feel foolish? In a time of betrayals, was this to be yet another one?

Blackthorn stood smiling down at him. It was a shrewd smile, wise, a little too cunning for Max's liking, not a smile to be comfortable with. It dared him to fathom some point that was beyond his depth, a point that — like a beginning swimmer — he could test only by letting go the side of the pool, submerging himself, feeling nothing underfoot. "I don't think I follow you," he said, looking up at Blackthorn. He was beginning to wish he'd played the Chopin waltz better; then none of this would have happened.

"What I've told you, Maximilian, might be called a parable. It may be true. Then again, it may be pure fiction. Now you're not sure which, are you?"

"No."

"And you may never know, Max. Never. Am I driving you slightly crazy with these thoughts? Are you beginning to feel a loss of balance?"

"Yes," said Max, increasingly unhappy about this turn in the conversation.

"Splendid! You see, Max, whether the story I've told you about myself is true or not . . . the point is, you must never take people and events at face value. You're accustomed to a life that comes delivered in neat packages. But now that you're twelve . . . and soon to be a man, according to your religious tradition . . . you must become *un*accustomed to that. I repeat, Max: life is messy. And unless you intend to become a recluse and hole up somewhere in Tibet, you must learn to do some fancy zig-zagging in this world. As in the case of your poor unpredictable rabbi. He's made an error that's human. Now Max, you must be divine, you must forgive him."

Without so much as a pause for breath, Blackthorn added: "Now let's hear the C-Sharp Minor as Chopin intended it to

be played. *One*-two-three *one*-two-three — "
Maximilian swung round on the piano bench and began.
This time it sounded more like a waltz.

15

All the way home Maximilian pondered the chronicle told him by his piano teacher. Was it pure fiction? Could it have been true?

By the time he reached his front porch he had made up his mind: the story *had* to be true. The proof was in the man's face, Derek Blackthorn's real autobiography. It took no stretch of Max's imagination to envision all the doors that had been shut in that face, all the heartless seaports and mean inland towns around the globe that had carved lines of hardship into it.

Not only did the boy find the tale believable, he found it strangely exciting. For Maximilian Glick, raised in a house where the fork was always placed here, the knife there, where one never entered without wiping one's feet (even on a perfect summer day), the idea that life was an endless series of mishaps made endurable by sporadic driblets of sanity . . . that idea was novel. More than novel. Amusing. Unsettling. Even scary. But undeniably exciting!

Max set down his music books on a table in the entrance hall.

"Max, is that you?"

It was his mother, calling from the livingroom.

"Yes — "

"Come into the livingroom, Max, please."

Maximilian now stood at the entrance to the livingroom. Next to the fireplace stood his mother and father, calm but grim. On the chesterfield sat a man whom Max had never before seen. Despite the generous upholstery on the chesterfield, the man was obviously uncomfortable. He sat stiffly, holding a fedora on his lap, as if he had come for only a short time and was determined to leave at the earliest possible moment. Max noticed that the man had pale gray eyes. In his formal-looking dark overcoat, he had the look of a retired bodyguard, or a detective, a man who could easily look after himself in the darkest alleys of any city. He looked at Maximilian and nodded, without smiling, without a word.

There was an awkward pause.

Then Sarah Glick stepped forward.

"Maxie," she said, "this is Mr. Brzjinski. He has something to say to you."

Mr. Brzjinski stood, revealing himself to be even taller and more muscular than Maximilian had imagined.

"How do you do, young man," he said, his voice deep and gravelly. "Your supper is waiting and so is mine. So I'll come right to the point. Like they say, short and sweet — "

The message Celia Brzjinski's father had come to convey was short. But it was not sweet. Not to Maximilian Glick's ears.

Celia Brzjinski's father and mother wanted no more of these foolish notions running through their daughter's head about a career in music, about going off to some fancy school in that jungle known as New York City. Celia had been raised in a God-fearing home. Her oldest brother was studying for the priesthood. Some day, when their daughter was finished high school, she would acquire a degree in something sensible, like nursing at Steelton General or teaching at the community college in Nickel City. None of this nonsense about "Brzjinski and Glick" would have arisen, said Papa Brzjinski, if that crazy Englishman had stuck to his business. His business, according to Celia's father, was to teach the girl to pedal better, no more, no less. From now on, Mr. Brzjinski announced, Celia would be continuing her piano lessons with Miss Klemenhoog, her old teacher, the one with the big feet.

When he'd finished saying what he had to say, Mr. Brzjinski turned toward Henry and Sarah Glick, bowed his massive head curtly, and muttered "Goodnight."

He brushed past Maximilian at the entrance to the living-room, and without looking up or saying another word let himself out of the house.

How had Celia Brzjinski's father learned of the secret?

"I don't believe in lying to you, Maximilian," said Henry Glick, providing the answer. "Your mother and I were very disturbed about this matter. Your grandmother calls it puppy love, but in this day and age kids do so much more . . . know so much more . . . than your mother and I when we were young. Life can become so complicated, Maximilian. Do you understand?"

"No, I don't understand — "

"What your father's trying to say, Maxie, is that it's important to us to maintain a Jewish home, a Jewish identity. And Celia's parents feel exactly the same way about their religion and their cultural background."

"Besides," Henry Glick added, "the world is full of struggling musicians. The sidewalks of New York are littered with the broken dreams of kids like you and Celia." Henry Glick took his son by the shoulders and looked down earnestly into the boy's face. "Do you understand what we're saying to you, Maxie? Do you understand it's for your own good?"

What was the point of arguing, thought Maximilian. After all, there was only one of him, and two of them. *Three* if you counted Mr. Brzjinski.

"Please try to understand, Maxie," Sarah Glick said.

That night Maximilian lay awake for hours, thinking. He heard the clock atop the old town hall strike midnight, then one A.M., then two. He heard the familiar whistle from time to time drifting across the sleeping city from the plant, signaling yet another volcanic eruption from the towering blast furnace as ore and limestone and fire became molten iron. At half-past three his eyes, already heavy with yesterday's bad news, gave up the struggle to stay open.

Some time around four in the morning Maximilian Glick found himself at a three-ring circus, in a tent jammed with spectators busy digging into boxes of popcorn, jabbering, spilling mustard on themselves from hotdogs, spilling orange drinks from paper cups, reaching, grabbing, laughing. Suddenly a shrill whistle cut through the din, jolting the unruly crowd into silence. It was the ringmaster, standing in the center of the ring, demanding everyone's attention as he introduced the circus acts. Max caught sight of his face, pink and shining under powerful overhead spotlights; it was the face of his gym teacher, Mr. Tipton-Thomas! Splendid in a red cutaway coat and white riding breeches, the ringmaster doffed his high black silk hat and, waving it with a flourish, gestured toward the outer ring to his right. "In this ring, ladies and gentlemen, boys and girls, we have. . . ."

Now he waved the hat in the direction of the outer ring to his left. "And in this ring we have. . . ."

Finally he extended his arms to take in the center ring. "And in *this* ring I give you. . . ."

The star attraction in each ring was the same . . . Maximilian Glick!

"Impossible!" people in the audience began to whisper, then to shout.

"Nothing is impossible," the ringmaster shouted back at them. "Watch!" The ringmaster turned to Maximilian Glick in Ring One and nodded, indicating that the show should begin. He gave the same signal in turn to Maximilian Glick in Ring Two and Ring Three.

All three Maximilian Glicks immediately launched into their acts.

In Ring One, Maximilian heard the alarm clock go off; heard his father call "Time to get up, Maxie"; drank his juice; ate his toast and peanut butter; grabbed his schoolbooks; ran a few steps to his classroom; dashed to the blackboard; multiplied 39,758 by 6743, divided the result by 15,334 — all in his head! — and chalked the correct answer on the blackboard in five seconds flat; turned and put on a long black academic robe and cap; took up a parchment scroll tied with a blue ribbon; untied the ribbon and read aloud: "Maximilian Glick is hereby awarded an Honorary Degree in Surgery, Chartered Accountancy and Judging, not to mention Auto Mechanics, Family Counseling, Plumbing and Electrical Repairs, and Aeronautical Engineering. ..."

In Ring Two, the young star was playing two grand pianos at once, hopping from one keyboard to the next, then sitting between them and playing one keyboard with his right hand, the other with his left; sometimes he seemed actually to have four hands and four feet.

Now there were four grand pianos and Maximilian Glick was playing all of them simultaneously while, on a podium at the center of the instruments, Sir Basil Blackthorn stood waving a long white baton. Suddenly the grand pianos began to split, each into two, then into four, until finally there were dozens of grand pianos and Maximilian was playing them all.

In the meantime, in Ring One, he was removing a brain tumor from a patient on an operating table, calculating an enormous bill for his medical services on a computer covered with levers and blinking lights, and banging a heavy wooden gavel on the bench as someone called out "Order in the court ... Judge Glick is now about to pronounce sentence on the accused!"

Over in Ring Three, Maximilian Glick was performing an entirely different act, and with remarkable energy, considering that he was already busy beyond belief in the other two rings. Here he was wearing a tallis, a prayer shawl, over his shoulders, and tefillin, traditional little leather boxes containing scriptures that were placed on the left arm and on the forehead between the eyes. On his head was a silver yarmulke, a skullcap, that caught the rays of the overhead lights and reflected them dazzlingly into the spectators' eyes. He was chanting in Hebrew a portion of the Torah from the Book of Numbers. "From the tribe of Reuben there were 46,500 ... the tribe of Simeon, 59,300 ... the tribe of Gad, 74,600. ..."
The audience marveled at his memory. There were gasps of

amazement, especially when at one point he began to chant in three voices, his own boyish tenor, Rabbi Kaminsky's resonant baritone, and a third vocal range that had the high-pitched intensity of the Lubavitcher rabbi....

Back to Ring One: Maximilian Glick has now removed two brain tumors, three spleens, and eleven appendixes, and he hasn't even had lunch yet! He has also totaled a column of figures as broad and as long as the two-lane highway stretching all the way from Steelton to Nickel City. And he has sentenced eighteen convicted criminals to prison and let off three others with suspended sentences and stern warnings. He is about to hear his twenty-second case, a man charged with criminal negligence. "Read the charge, Clerk," says Judge Glick. The court clerk rises and reads aloud: "Your Honor, this man is charged with keeping a loose, disorderly, and dangerous tongue in his mouth, and allowing it to escape on the night of...."

The ringmaster looks triumphant as the audience applauds and cheers wildly. Microphone in hand, he calls out to the star in the rings: "*Run* Maximilian, *jump* Maximilian; *operate*, *calculate*, *adjudicate* Maximilian! ... *Play* Maximilian, *pray* Maximilian! ..."

In the bleachers Morris Moskover declares: "The boy's a natural wonder, and that's all there is to it!" Two seats away, Amos Kerkorian is busy taking credit for having supplied groceries to the Boy Wonder all these years. Sarah and Henry Glick stand and take a bow. Now the spotlight shifts from them to Augustus and Bryna Glick and they too stand and take a bow, Augustus waving grandly like a monarch, Bryna blowing kisses like an opera star.

Back again to Ring One: The court clerk is still reading the same charge: "And furthermore, Your Honor, this man is charged with committing treason by betraying a sacred confidence...."

Suddenly the audience is hushed. Only the voice of the clerk is heard, droning on with the list of charges: "And furthermore, the accused is said to have become intoxicated in public...."

"Do you have a lawyer?" Judge Glick asks, glaring down

from the bench at the miserable accused.

"I am my own lawyer," replies the accused man.

"Then you are a fool twice, for a lawyer who defends himself has a fool for a lawyer and a fool for a client. Guilty as charged!"

The man in the prisoner's dock begins to protest. "But you can't condemn me, Your Honor. You haven't heard my defence. You have not given me the fair trial to which every man is entitled...."

The ringmaster calls out: "Maximilian, be fair, be just. Maximilian, you must do what is right — "

"Guilty!" declares Maximilian Glick, accentuating this verdict by pounding his gavel.

The poor man in the dock cries out: "Justice! Mercy! It was only a mistake. To err is human, Your Honor — "

"Maximilian, forgive!" orders the ringmaster.

But something is going wrong in the three rings.

In Ring One Judge Glick has put on his black hat, which means he is about to pronounce a very severe sentence upon the unhappy man who stands before the bench in shackles. Will it be death?

In Ring Two there are now hundreds of grand pianos all playing Mozart's Sonata No. 3 in different keys, and the music sounds as though it was composed at a convention of devils and madmen.

In Ring Three the chanting boy in the prayer shawl and skullcap seems to have gone haywire, like a computer full of short-circuits. "From the tribe of Blatherblather, 89,487,793 ... from the tribe of Mumbojumbo, 119,748,482...." The numbers became more and more preposterous.

"What is happening?" the ringmaster asks himself. He is losing control of the circus. In each ring the star has got out of hand, the act has gone crazy. The audience is becoming uneasy, fearful. They are beginning to eye the exits.

Frowning, the ringmaster consults his program. No, this was definitely *not* on the schedule. He summons his assistant and whispers: "Tell Maximilian Glick he is not playing the game, not sticking to the contract. Tell him he'll never work in this circus or any *other* circus again unless — "

But it's too late.

In Ring One, Case No. 22 has just been disposed of. The prisoner has been sentenced. Banishment for life outside the Gates of the World. The guards, two burly men who resemble furniture movers, are stripping the accused man of his uniform — a black hat, black frock coat, black shoes. The man is forced to put on a clown's costume, constructed of patches of cloth containing every color known to man, complete with matching hat and shoes. "Take him away!" orders the judge.

In shame, the new clown is led away to his banishment.

The judge smiles with satisfaction.

Sputtering angrily, the ringmaster shouts: "No! No! This was not called for. This was not expected, Maximilian. You *must* not do the unexpected. It is simply out of the question."

"Call the next case," the judge says, ignoring the furious ringmaster.

"Case No. 23 — " The court clerk, also satisfied with the way things are going, smiles at the judge. The court clerk is a girl. She is about twelve or thirteen, a bit tall for her age but with excellent posture, a kind of elegance despite her youth. Her resemblance to Celia Brzjinski is remarkable.

By now the ringmaster is beside himself with rage. He has lost control of the three-ring circus. In one of the rings a tail is wagging a dog; a tree is shaking the wind; a birthday cake is suspended in mid-air, upside-down, with countless candles burning, their flames shooting downward like rocket trails. "Impossible! *Impossible!*" the ringmaster cries.

"Nothing is impossible," Maximilian Glick cries back.

"Impossible! — " This time it was the voice of Henry Glick. "I must have forgotten to set the alarm last night. Wake up Maxie. It's a quarter past eight. We've all slept in. Hurry, or you'll be late for school."

With the bone-weariness of a young man who had just spent an entire night performing all three acts in a three-ring circus, Maximilian got slowly out of bed and raised his window blind. Though it was the first day of March, he had expected to see the gray overcast sky of a typical February morning, for February had a way of locking Steelton in its grip, sometimes holding it there until well into April.

To the boy's astonishment, the sun was shining in a cloudless sky. On the eaves of the old house icicles were dripping their way into extinction. Except for the snow on the ground, he could have sworn it *was* a day in April.

"Maxie, it's late — " Henry Glick was calling up to him again. "Are you out of bed? Maxie?"

"I'm up, I'm up," the boy called back.

Maximilian stared at the sky and the sun again.

Something told him this was going to be a strange day. An unusual day. A day full of the *un*expected.

16

Through the only window in his livingroom, Rabbi Teitelman too saw that March had arrived in its own way, warm and sunny, with seemingly no ties whatever to the heartless month just ended.

Looking down into the yard behind the apartment building, he saw another sight that was unexpected. His landlady, Mrs. MacWatters, was feverishly engaged in what appeared to be early spring cleaning.

Normally a gentle person who spoke with a soft Scottish brogue, Mrs. MacWatters was noisily and vigorously beating several small rugs, shaking a blanket until it flapped and slapped, punching a large pillow as if it were a sparring partner and she were going for a knockout in the first round. Amused by the sight of such violence, all done in the name of good housekeeping, the Lubavitcher rabbi opened his window. "Good morning, Mrs. MacWatters," he called down.

Mrs. MacWatters gave the pillow a moment's respite from her punishing blows. "Good morning, Rabbi," she responded cheerfully. "It's a beautiful morning. You must have said some special prayers for good weather."

The rabbi laughed. "I've been praying for decent weather since last November."

"Sometimes it takes the dear Lord a bit longer to hear prayers from Steelton. You have to say them quickly or they freeze before they reach His ears, you know."

"I didn't know that," admitted Rabbi Teitelman. "Thank you for the tip."

"I'll give you another tip, Rabbi," said Mrs. MacWatters in her Scottish brogue. "If you intend to get your share of this sunshine you'd better get it quickly. One never knows what the next hour will bring in this part of the country."

"Good idea," said the rabbi. "But first, *I'm* going to do a little spring cleaning too."

Rabbi Teitelman went to his desk, checked his daily diary, and saw that he had no appointments until mid-afternoon. Perfect. That would give him an opportunity to follow his landlady's lead.

Covering his slight frame in an oversized flannel bathrobe, he went into the backyard where he proceeded to hang up on the clothesline his long frock coat, his black suit including jacket, pants, and vest, as well as several other garments that needed daylight and fresh air after months of confinement in his closet. To be certain they were secure in the event of a sudden stiff breeze, he buttoned the coat, jacket, and vest, and checked the hangers carefully. With the aid of two stout clothes pegs he fastened his wide-brimmed black hat to the line. A pull at the brim of the hat, a tug at the hem of the jacket satisfied him that all was in order, and he retired to his small apartment.

From his bookshelf he withdrew an old leather-bound book, sat himself in his rocking chair, and began to study the commentaries for the Torah portion he was to read at the next Sabbath morning service.

Through the window, which he had left open, an unseasonably balmy breeze drifted into the room. It ruffled the thin pages of the text, tumbling the words gently and rolling them into a blurry ball. In a moment the young rabbi's head drooped, his red beard fanned out across his chest, and he was fast asleep.

He hadn't intended to sleep at all, for there was plenty of work to do. The Torah portion had to be studied; a sermon had to be written; there were test papers to be marked in time for the cheder class later that day. And most troubling of all, Maximilian Glick was due at four for another bar mitzvah lesson. It would be the first meeting between rabbi and pupil since the débâcle at Maximilian's home.

Over and over again, since that event, Maximilian's words had echoed in the rabbi's ears. "You're not my friend...." Hourly, with the regularity of the clock atop the town hall, Rabbi Teitelman had berated himself for what had happened, and pondered various ways to restore his relationship with Maximilian. Should he have a long talk with the Glicks? Should he have a long talk with Maximilian? He had already had several long talks with God, but these gave him little comfort and no solutions. What to do?

In the meantime, his nights had been restless. And so now, seated in his rocking chair, with the heavy volume lying open across his lap, he slumbered, his cares nudged into the background by a steady rhythmic snore.

But not for long.

Something — probably a particularly loud snore — acted as an alarm, jolting the rabbi awake. He glanced toward the open window where the thin curtains flailed the air like angry tentacles, fanned by a storm that was supposed to bypass Steelton but apparently changed its mind at the last moment. "Oh my God!" the rabbi whispered. Still in his bathrobe, he dashed down a flight of stairs to fetch his garments.

But the hat, the pants, the vest, the frock coat ... gone, each and every one of them.

Feeling ridiculous in his bathrobe and slippers, the rabbi knocked frantically on Mrs. MacWatters' door. Had she seen what had become of his clothes, hung out in the yard? — No.

Within moments the landlady was on the telephone to the police.

Moments after that, a reporter from the *Steelton Star*, assigned to cover police headquarters, caught the scent of the story and was on the phone to his city editor. "Joe," said the reporter to his boss, "you're always complaining that I don't come up with unusual human-interest stuff. Have I got a story for you!"

The afternoon edition of the *Star* carried the tale of the

rabbi's missing wardrobe on the front page, dead center, and by dinnertime, on several thousand television screens in Steelton, there was Mrs. MacWatters in her Sunday going-to-church coat, green cloth with a genuine fox collar, pointing to the clothesline in the backyard, explaining to reporters in her Highland accent her theory as to how precisely the clothes had disappeared. "Anything could have happened, and did," said Mrs. MacWatters.

With this explanation the reporters would have to be satisfied, for the "hero" of the story — the rabbi himself — declined to be interviewed. After canceling his appointments for the day, the rabbi agreed that he would see a police inspector, but no one else.

At the bakery next morning, Cal Irwin and his cronies jokingly accused each other of the theft. Irwin pointed to Doc Larue, the optometrist, who sat three stools away in a white cotton jacket. "I bet that black coat's a darn sight cleaner than the one you got on!" Everybody, including Doc Larue, roared with laughter.

In the hotel beverage rooms and the pool halls, men who had never outgrown Hallowe'en engaged in similar joking accusations. But in these places, ribaldry and truth often went hand in hand. One never knew for certain if one drank or played a billiard shot in company with a harmless prankster, or a man with a criminal record the size of a phone book.

Two days passed, and no sign of the missing garments. No clues. No confessions. The rabbi, in the meantime, having no suitable clothes to wear in substitution for the ones that had disappeared, remained in seclusion in his small apartment. What little food he required Mrs. MacWatters was kind enough to purchase for him at Kerkorian's. He slept little, and spent most of his waking hours in his bathrobe and slippers, his skullcap crowning his head of red hair like a black mountain peak.

The rabbi's congregation, in the meantime, became divided and quarrelsome over the matter.

Some were sympathetic to the young Lubavitcher. They

understood how much the traditional hat and frock coat meant to him. They understood that a Lubavitcher did not simply shrug and say, "Oh well, I'll just wear something else."

Others took the opposite view however — men like Harry Zwicker and Milt Katzenberg who hadn't been happy about the Lubavitcher since that first moment he'd stepped off the airport bus — and Augustus Glick who would gladly have sent him packing months ago.

"We are now the laughing stock of the town," Harry Zwicker declared bitterly. Many heads in the congregation nodded in agreement, including that of Zelig Peikes. In fact, Peikes recalled, this was the first occasion in more than twenty years that a hostile act had been committed against any Jew in Steelton.

"They never would have done this before the Lubavitcher came to town," said Milt Katzenberg.

One voice rose to challenge Katzenberg. It was Morris Moskover, the Local Sage. "They?" said Moskover. "Who's 'they'?"

But Katzenberg had little use for sages, and for Moskover in particular. "They. . . . *Them.* Who else?"

Moskover screwed an index finger high into the air, his favorite gesture when about to make a point. "How do you know it was not one of *us*?" he asked.

This suggestion ignited the circle of Jews within hearing. Cries of "Shame!" rained down on Morris Moskover like fragments of a bomb.

"I still say it's a distinct possibility," Moskover retorted.

Pointing accusingly at the Local Sage, Katzenberg shouted: "Then it must have been *you* Moskover." Katzenberg, of course, didn't believe this for a moment. But it was one way to stifle the man and it succeeded. Morris Moskover said nothing more.

After three days of diligent search, the police turned up not a thread, not a button.

Deeply troubled, the police inspector assigned to the case, Wilbur Barnswell, prepared to call upon Rabbi Teitelman to report failure.

A veteran with twenty-five years' experience, Inspector Barnswell was totally baffled by the case of the missing rabbinical property. Local crimes tended to be committed by ordinary wrongdoers doing ordinary wrongs — vagrancy, drunkenness, common assault. More often than not the culprits were caught red-handed; more often than not there wasn't the slightest mystery about their crimes; investigation, arrest, and judgment followed in swift sequence, permitting Inspector Barnswell ample time to indulge in his first love — growing prize roses.

"I'm sorry to have to say this, Rabbi, but we haven't uncovered a single clue," Inspector Barnswell confessed.

"Is there anything more to be done?" Rabbi Teitelman asked calmly.

"I could post a reward for information leading — "

The rabbi interrupted. "Rewards only God can grant."

The inspector thought a moment. "I have sources . . . two or three people who frequent the hotel beverage rooms, the pool halls, that sort of place. Occasionally they come up with something useful."

Politely the rabbi again objected. "I would find the use of information distasteful in this case. Anyway, it's possible that my things were carried off by the sudden storm. And who in the City of Steelton is so bold as to inform on the winds?"

Never having dealt with a Lubavitcher rabbi in his twenty-five years on the police force, Inspector Barnswell wasn't quite certain he understood this last question. "It doesn't matter," said the rabbi, still calm. "I have made other plans." He thanked the inspector, blessed him for his concern, and saw him to the door.

On the fourth day following the disappearance, Gerry O'Grady, proprietor of the largest used car business in Steelton, stood at the open door of the small frame one-room building that housed his office, idly surveying the inventory on his graveled lot. At the far end he noticed a man strolling between the rows of cars. The man was wearing a heavy fisherman's cardigan over a turtleneck sweater, and dark corduroy pants. On his head was a black knitted seaman's cap, pulled well down at the sides to cover his ears against the cold; concealing much of his forehead, it left enough, just enough red hair showing that, taken together with the red beard, there could be little mistake about who the caller was.

Not quite able to believe his eyes, O'Grady put on his eyeglasses and peered again. Then he stepped from the open door. "Good afternoon, Rabbi," he called.

"Good afternoon. Are you the owner of this establishment?"

"I like to tell people this is my lot in life." O'Grady smiled, advancing toward the visitor.

They met over the hood of a 1976 Pontiac. The rabbi studied Gerry O'Grady's face, a wide-open territory free of shadowy and suspicious crevices. Rabbi Teitelman decided that Gerry O'Grady was the kind of man from whom one *would* buy a used car.

"I'm looking for a reasonably good car," said the rabbi.

"Going somewhere?"

"Isn't everyone?" Even with Gentiles the young Lubavitcher more often than not answered one question with another.

"You looking for basic transportation?"

"What else is a car for?"

They walked together past several ranks of cars, like officers inspecting a company of infantrymen. At last the rabbi touched Gerry O'Grady's arm. He pointed to a small Japanese sports car, about five years old. Black, of course.

"That's a snappy little number," said the used car dealer, "but it's kind of small, isn't it?"

"Why do I need big?" asked the rabbi.

"Maybe you oughta try it out first, Rabbi. I gotta be honest with you; sometimes the first owners of cars like these drive the devil out of them, if you'll pardon the expression."

"What could be more appropriate for a clergyman!" said the rabbi with enthusiasm.

While O'Grady made out the bill of sale, the young Lubavitcher smiled to himself. The idea of driving a car from which the devil had been cast out appealed to him almost as much as the low cost. O'Grady, a man of conscience, had discounted the sale price after confessing that only God knew how long the transmission would hold up.

By nightfall the rabbi had fitted his books nicely into the trunk of the small black car. A lone suitcase containing some clothing and a cardboard carton holding personal papers shared the passenger seat. The rabbi looked under his bed, checked his dresser drawers, ran his eyes over the bookshelves and desk in the livingroom, carried out a final inspection of the kitchen and bathroom cabinets. Satisfied that he'd packed everything he needed, he locked the apartment door behind him, slid the key under Mrs. MacWatters' door, climbed behind the wheel of his new used car, and drove off.

On the edge of town he stopped only long enough to let the astonished attendant at an all-night service station fill the tank and check the oil. Then the little Japanese sports car gave a lurch and sped away, carrying the Lubavitcher rabbi into the night.

17

Staring moodily out the bay window at the slate-gray St. Anne, just beyond a raw patch of scrub and wild grass that separated his house from the river, Derek Blackthorn drew a heavy cardigan tighter around his hunched shoulders and shuddered. "The revenge of April on the human race," he growled in a Shakespearean voice. "April ... bastard child of spring and summer, claimed by both, disowned by both ... this frowning month of everlasting mists. ..." Thick clouds now dipped so close to the water's surface that they seemed about to blot the river dry. "Just look at that sky, Max. Shall we never see the sun again?"

Maximilian, seated at the piano, head bent over the keyboard, showed not the slightest interest. He was only half-listening, so lost was he in his own thoughts — thoughts made gloomier by the sound of rainwater dripping from the Blackthorns' rusted eavestroughs, slowly, steadily, like the measured beat of time itself.

Without taking his eyes from the scene outside, Blackthorn asked quietly: "You're sure your decision is final ... no chance you might change your mind?"

Again the boy remained silent. Blackthorn turned and looked at him. "Max? — "

Max nodded. "No chance," he said in a low voice.

"I see." After a moment's pause, the teacher crossed the room and stood directly behind his pupil. Reaching over the boy's shoulder, he poked a skeletal index finger into the sheet of music open above the keyboard. "Know what I think, Glick?"

he said, trying to josh. "You've allowed yourself to become spooked by just the *look* of the piece. Now, it does, I grant you, resemble something Spot and Rover might have dragged in after a night of carousing on the town ... all those killer-octaves and knuckle-cracking chords. And the key ... my God, Max, five flats!" Blackthorn waited for some reaction from his pupil, but none was forthcoming. Forcing himself to be chipper, he went on: "Well, that's a Liszt étude for you. Coronary music I call it. Never play Liszt without a doctor in the house!" Still no sign of life from Max. "Look, Maximilian," Blackthorn brightened, "I *could* try ringing up the publisher ... see if it's possible to have the piece re-issued in something more palatable ... say, the key of F. That's only one flat. Of course, old Franz'll turn over in his tomb, but it's time he saw the other view, anyway. Besides, it's the *tune* that counts, I always say. What do you always say?"

"It doesn't really matter."

"What doesn't really matter, Max?"

"What key it's in. I'm not going to enter the festival. Not this year. Not any year, maybe."

"You mean ... because you might have to compete against Celia?"

As if defending the girl's honor, Max shot a resentful look at his teacher. "Celia would never ... I mean, she swore if *I* didn't, *she* wouldn't either."

Blackthorn chuckled cynically. "Oh, is that so?" he said. "Well, I've news for you, my friend. At this very moment Miss Brzjinski is well into the Concert Etude No. 3 — five flats and all — presumably with Madame Klemenhoog and Papa Brzjinski hovering over her like midwives at a lying-in."

"I don't believe it. She gave me her word."

"Ah, but she didn't give you her *father's* word, and in that family, it's his that counts, apparently."

Max gave his teacher a skeptical look. "How do you know all this?"

"Simple, Max. It came from *the* unimpeachable source — Agnes Moore."

No more needed to be said. The boy understood immediately. Agnes Moore ran Steelton's only music shop, a clearing house for local cultural gossip (including what *really* went on in the mansion of Mrs. Gabor-Mindesz after everyone, except a certain handsome cellist, left her soirées). If one wanted to know who was playing what, and with whom, anywhere within a hundred miles of Moore's Music Store, one had only to compliment the lady on her latest handwoven shawl (always the color of cooked oatmeal) and say something in French to Gaston, her white poodle.

Blackthorn brought his face close to Max's. "Now then, won't you snap out of this . . . this silliness?"

"It's *not* silliness," Max insisted hotly.

"I'm sorry, Max," Blackthorn said quickly, backing off. "I oughtn't to have put it that way. Please forgive me."

Returning to the bay window, Blackthorn leaned the palms of his hands against the cold glass. For a full minute the room was locked in a strained silence. Then, without warning, Blackthorn swung round and, flinging all diplomacy to the April wind, shouted: "No no no! I bloody well refuse to stand by and let you do this to yourself, Max. All the hundreds and hundreds of hours you've worked and sweated . . . what about *them*? What about New York? . . . Juilliard? What will you do instead, carry a towel and water bucket for the likes of Sandy Siltaanen? Hang around the bakery after school with the likes of Bobby Rosenberg? Deliver pizzas for Frank Senior's?"

"Maybe," the boy mumbled.

"Is that all you can say, *maybe*?" Blackthorn raged. "I've put four years of my life into you, Max. Four hard . . . long — " Blackthorn broke off and turned away, shaking his head bitterly.

"I'm sorry," said Max in a voice barely audible. Without another word, he got up from the piano bench. Avoiding his teacher's accusing gaze, he gathered up his jacket and scarf in a careless ball and, without stopping to put them on, started out of the room. At the double doors that led to the entrance hall he tried to repeat "I'm sorry," but the words stuck to his tongue.

Maximilian made his way along the wet street with angry strides, feeling every inch the victim, mocked, betrayed, bereft of the thing closest to him — his private dreams. The wind off the river buffeted him, working its damp fingers up and down his back, but he was oblivious to it until, at last, bone-cold and defeated now even by the elements, he was forced to stop in his tracks to don his jacket and scarf. Looking up defiantly at the overcast skies, he called aloud: "Teitelman ... I hope you're satisfied. *Damn* you, Teitelman ... wherever you are!"

Wherever he was ... that was indeed the question.

Where was Kalman Teitelman?

18

In the weeks following his disappearance, the Lubavitcher rabbi's whereabouts had become the mystery on everyone's lips.

Though the service station attendant observed that the small Japanese car was definitely heading north when he last saw it, none of the townspeople along that stretch of highway reported the appearance of a vehicle matching the description of the rabbi's, nor had anyone seen a stranger resembling the driver himself.

For once, Zelig Peikes, the president of the congregation, Harry Zwicker, the secretary, and Milt Katzenberg, the treasurer, were unanimous about something. "He must have turned around and headed south," reasoned Zelig Peikes, and the others agreed.

To the Jews of Steelton, "South" always meant Toronto, and south was indeed the logical direction for a man like Kalman Teitelman to go. South was where there were Jewish schools, Jewish libraries and museums, synagogues so large you needed field glasses to see the rabbi in his pulpit. If you were sick, there was a Jewish hospital equipped like a luxury hotel. There was even a Jewish Y — in fact, *two* Jewish Y's, one for the uptown athletes, one for the downtown athletes.

You could be a sidewalk Jew in the south. There were whole sections of the city where one saw nothing but Jewish butcher shops and fish markets and bakeries, Jewish bookstores, restaurants, and variety shops.

And then there were study houses where a Lubavitcher scholar, starved for the company of other scholars after months of isolation in some northern wilderness, could find rich food for the mind and a hot strong cup of tea with lots of lemon and sugar for the body.

And most importantly, there were tailorshops where a Lubavitcher rabbi could find with ease exactly what he needed to replenish his traditional wardrobe.

"Yes, he *must* be in Toronto," said Zelig Peikes. "I'll drop a line to the Central Jewish Agency there. They must have heard from him by now."

"Never mind dropping a line," said Milt Katzenberg. "Call!"

Coming from Milt Katzenberg, the congregation's frugal treasurer, this was an extraordinary suggestion. Long distance calls were like champagne for breakfast and caviar at bedtime — shameful extravagances. He was the kind of treasurer who counted every postage stamp, every paperclip.

"Call!" Katzenberg repeated.

Harry Zwicker went even further. "Make *ten* calls if you have to," he said to Peikes. "God only knows what's happened to the poor man. Maybe he was hijacked."

"Maybe he was mugged," said Katzenberg, who loathed big cities. "You know what Toronto is like. Every second person on the streets is a professional mugger. I read it in the paper."

"Nonsense," said Zelig Peikes, who considered himself much more sophisticated about such matters. "My brother Walter Peikes the multi-millionaire has lived in Toronto all his life and he's never been mugged. Not once."

"That's because your brother the multi-millionaire hasn't bought himself a new suit since the Second World War," said Katzenberg.

"Let's not waste time," shouted Harry Zwicker. "Call, for Godsakes!" Zwicker's sense of urgency reflected the anxiety of the entire congregation, for even the Lubavitcher's sharpest critics were by this time deeply concerned about the young man's safety.

Peikes called the Agency. No, they hadn't heard so much as a word from Rabbi Teitelman.

The Agency in turn called a number of places in the city where a Lubavitcher might be found. The response was always the same: Kalman Teitelman? No, the name didn't ring any bells. What did he look like? Red-headed? Thin and pale? Why, there were *dozens* of young Lubavitchers matching that description in Toronto. Easier to identify a wave in the ocean, a pebble on the beach!

In desperation, the Agency called the rabbi's parents in Boston. This turned out to be a grave mistake. Informed that their son had apparently disappeared, the elder Teitelmans began to weep and wail on the other end of the line, and the director of the Agency began to wish his fingers had become paralysed a moment before he'd dialed their number.

As time went by, it seemed that every man, woman, and child in Steelton had some tale or other about where the Lubavitcher was supposed to be, about what he was supposed to be doing.

Harry Zwicker's cousin, who lived on a kibbutz in Israel, wrote Zwicker that a Kalman Teitelman from the United States was now residing at a neighboring kibbutz near the Lebanese border, teaching English to children by day, leading a crack company of marksmen on guard duty by night.

Abe Resnick, who sold machinery and tools to logging companies, heard from a number of his customers that the Lubavitcher — minus beard and wearing a heavy mackinaw jacket and steel-toed boots — was spotted operating a bulldozer deep in the timber country north of Thunder Bay. According to the loggers, he lived in a roominghouse and took most of his meals at a highway truckstop run by an attractive middle-aged widow who was constantly serving him second helpings of dessert "on the house."

Gerry O'Grady, of O'Grady's Honest-To-Goodness Used Cars, came across a magazine advertisement by an Italian car manufacturer showing one of its sports models being tested over a rugged mountain pass in Switzerland. He told a reporter for the *Steelton Star* that the man behind the wheel was none other than the man to whom he had sold the little black Japanese two-seater. "No doubt about it," said O'Grady.

The proprietor of the Harborside Motel said he'd swear on all the Gideon Bibles in his motel that he'd seen the Lubavitcher sporting a neat red mustache and working as a bell captain at a large convention hotel in Las Vegas.

Not to be outdone, Morris Moskover proclaimed that *all* the stories were accurate. "The man is everywhere, and that's all there is to it," he said.

Ever mindful of his presidential duties, and with his eye fixed at all times on the next election, Zelig Peikes — with the assistance of the Central Jewish Agency — hired a new rabbi for Steelton's Jewish congregation.

"He's the right man for us," said Peikes. "He's forty, has one wife, two kids, wears a three-piece suit, and drives a four-door car."

"Yes yes," said Milt Katzenberg impatiently, "but what's he *look* like?"

"Like a lawyer, thank God!" replied Peikes.

When news of the hiring of a new rabbi was announced at the Glick dinnertable one evening, Bryna Glick once again found herself in the minority. "I still feel we let Rabbi Teitelman down," said she. "You have to admit that he made all of us a little more conscious of our old-country values, a little less anxious to be like everybody else, to blend in with the woodwork, so to speak."

"With all due respect," said Sarah Glick, "any man who deserts his post because his uniform's been stolen or has simply vanished is not much of a man in my eyes."

Augustus Glick couldn't miss an opportunity to needle his wife a bit. "I remember when you promoted him from corporal to captain ... on Yom Kippur night, when he passed out after blowing the shofar."

"Well, as far as I'm concerned, he's still a captain," Bryna retorted.

Henry Glick disagreed. "I'll admit that he made us pull up our socks when it came to things like attending services regularly, observing certain rules and regulations, details of that sort. But men like him really don't belong in the twentieth century, I'm afraid."

"But what about the hundreds, even thousands, of Lubavitchers in the big cities — New York, Montreal, Chicago?" Bryna said. "Surely you're not going to sit there and tell me they all belong to some other time, or on some other planet?"

"That's different, with all due respect," Sarah Glick explained. "You see, in a metropolis like New York they have each other. They don't stand out like oddballs, the way this young man did here."

Bryna Glick, having been addressed with all due respect twice in less than five minutes, could feel a small inner flame setting fire to her temper. "Sarah my dear," she said to her daughter-in-law, "when Augustus and I first came to Steelton in the early Twenties, didn't we look more than a little 'oddball'?"

Augustus Glick sat up. "I *beg* your pardon, my dear?"

"You've forgotten the pictures of the two of us when we'd just got off the boat from Europe. I wore a dress that looked like a torn parachute. And Augustus here wore a pair of pants that were so ragged and short they looked as if they'd been eaten away by mice."

Now old Augustus Glick rose to the defence. "Now see here, Bryna, if you're referring to the photographs that were taken in Halifax, I'll have you know that those trousers belonged to my Uncle Gottfried who served with distinction in the Horse Guard of the Austrian Army."

"I thought it was your grandfather that served with distinction in the Horse Guard," said Bryna.

Augustus stiffened his back like a soldier. "So he did. *And* my Uncle Gottfried. *And* several cousins as well. I come from a long line of fine loyal militiamen . . . men who were officers and gentlemen."

"But you still came to Canada in a pair of borrowed pants,"

Bryna Glick shot back.

Henry Glick took up arms now against Bryna. "I don't see what Dad's pants have to do with the Lubavitcher rabbi," he said. "Or your dress, for that matter."

With Henry, Augustus, and Sarah busy attacking on three flanks, and Bryna busy with counter-attacks, none of the Glicks noticed that Maximilian had discreetly slipped away from the dinnertable, leaving his food largely untouched.

In the peace and quiet of his bedroom, with the lights off, he stood at his window, looking out at the familiar landscape of Steelton.

Was it possible, he wondered, that the small city had somehow grown smaller? How long had it been since he had last taken the time to stand there, in his private lookout atop Pine Hill, surveying the city that lay below? Weeks? Months? A year?

Once again ships were moving in the St. Anne River, unconcerned about the odd little islands of ice that floated here and there, clinging to their sizes and shapes in the chilly spring night, but losing out little by little to the sun during the day. Except for the movement of the lake freighters, all of Steelton seemed to be plunged into stillness and darkness. There was life out there, to be sure. But in the "between" days and nights of a Steelton April, the local citizenry were not yet ready to unfold; instead, people still cherished the habits of winter — a fireplace with a blaze, the evening paper, the inevitable glow of the television set in the livingroom.

With June not that many weeks off, Maximilian would ordinarily have been at the piano at this hour, wrestling with Liszt's tortuous étude, cursing the key of D-flat under his breath, cursing the Hungarian, long since dead and buried, for planting a land mine in each and every bar of the composition, cursing the gentle committee of tea-drinking cookie-nibbling ladies of the festival auxiliary who, with the advice of outside experts like Professor Lacoste, drew up the syllabus of contest pieces. But not tonight. Tonight he could only think of Celia Brzjinski, several blocks away in that stone fortress, mastering page after page of octaves, chromatic runs, ascending thirds guaranteed to break the strongest fingernails. He could see her father winking sternly at her mother, giving a victory sign with his thick powerful fingers, reminding Celia in his chesty baritone that it was only eight-thirty and she had another hour to go, not that the girl needed reminding.

For no reason in particular, the boy began to recite his name aloud, slowly, over and over again — "Maximilian . . . Maximilian . . . Maximilian. . . ." Now twelve, he would be thirteen sooner than one would think, he told himself. Strange, he thought, how each day, taken by itself, seemed to drag on as if sundown would never happen; and yet, in the context of weeks, all the days seemed bunched up, hurled across the span from one season to the next like a meteor. Twelve, going on thirteen. Young. But old. "I must have been *born* old" — something Maximilian Glick had told himself many times over the short years of his life — now came back to him and he repeated it aloud to himself as he stood in the darkness looking out his window at the dark city. He wondered if he would ever get to stand at a different window, look out at a different city.

19

One morning early in June, Cal Irwin came into the bakery for morning coffee with his neighborhood cronies, who included Henry Glick. "You'll never believe what I saw last night on television!" said Irwin, in a state of great excitement. "You remember that young rabbi, the fellow with the red beard that blew out of town one night back in March?" Everyone nodded. Of course they remembered. Who could forget? "Well," Irwin continued, so eager to tell his story he ignored the waitress's request for his order, "I swear I saw him on the program from Los Angeles, you know the one, it's on every week ... where they give new comedians a chance to try out their act. He did this monologue, or whatever they call it, about how he grew up in Boston and had all these fantasies about going to strange places and doing strange things — "

"What was he wearing?" the baker smirked skeptically.

"Plaid sportshirt, open at the neck ... you could see the upper part of his T-shirt, y'know ... tweed jacket. Hey, and a pair of beat-up sneakers. But I'll swear it's the same guy. I forgot his name, but I tell you I never forget a face. Never!"

The others in the bakery scoffed. This was the most ridiculous tale yet. "All comedians look alike these days," said Henry Glick. "You can't tell 'em apart. Same clothes. Same jokes."

"Maybe," Irwin admitted reluctantly, "but there was something different about this guy." Then, chuckling, Irwin said: "He told this story about a bunch of Jewish folks who go down to this river at New Year's to dump out their pockets, like they're getting rid of their sins, see?" Irwin turned to Henry Glick. "There *is* such a custom among you folks, isn't there Henry?" Henry nodded yes, and Irwin smiled with satisfaction, his credibility now firmly established. "Anyway, these people are busy emptying their pockets, and one poor old gent, the poorest of the bunch, accidentally plunks his last ten-dollar bill into the water, just as the rabbi's preaching that it's a time for change. And the poor old gent" — Irwin interrupted himself to laugh — "the poor old gent yells out 'If it's all the same to you, rabbi, I'll take two fives.'"

Henry Glick assured Cal Irwin that a mouse would marry an elephant and have quintuplets before a Lubavitcher would be caught dead on late-night television, especially a comedy show.

That evening, at the dinnertable, Henry Glick related Cal Irwin's story to Sarah and Maximilian. Sarah laughed. "I like the joke," said she, "but really, the whole idea is preposterous." She and her husband agreed that the coincidence about the ten-dollar bill and Nathan Pripchick was remarkable, yes, but Rabbi Teitelman a standup comic on television? "No way," said Sarah, and she and Henry burst into laughter once again. Only then did Henry realize that his son was not joining in the mirth. "What's wrong, Maxie, don't you get it?" he asked. "You see, son, there's this old man and he's emptying his pockets — "

Suddenly Maximilian began to laugh.

"Wait a minute, Max," said his father earnestly, "I haven't come to the punchline yet."

"It's okay," said Maximilian, bringing his laughter under control, "I get it. Believe me, I get it." And pleading that he was too full to finish his dinner, the boy excused himself and hastened to the privacy of his room, feeling now as if he held deep within him the secret of life itself.

That night Maximilian Glick stood once again at his window, looking up at the night sky. Somewhere in the atmosphere it was possible that at this very moment a signal was being transmitted from a television studio, an indiscernible wave of light and sound which, unraveled through a labyrinth of wires and tubes, would become — incredibly! — the face and voice of Kalman Teitelman, or Kal Title, or whatever he had chosen to call himself.

The man had broken out. And now the boy knew that he too would break out some day. Tomorrow morning, he promised himself, he would call Derek Blackthorn ... first thing, before school. This year's festival, only a few days off now, was out of the question. But next year, Max whispered to himself ... *next year!*

And some day, somewhere, the Lubavitcher rabbi and he would meet again. Of that much, Maximilian was certain. Where precisely, and how? — Who knew? Perhaps on a stage, or in a studio, or in an airport half-way around the world, or in a city where the skyscrapers seemed to be reaching higher than their fixed heights, as if grasping for more than their share of the sun.

And then again, perhaps they would not meet in any real place, only in some spiritual territory where the line between what people are and what people dream of being is invisible, like a spider's first spinning.